T0065267

"I KNOW HOW TO STRUGGLE, I NEED TO KNOW HOW TO BE BLESSED"

BRENT J. ELLIS

"I KNOW HOW TO STRUGGLE, I NEED TO KNOW HOW TO BE BLESSED"

iUniverse books may be ordered through booksellers or by contacting:

iUniverse
1663 Liberty Drive
Bloomington, IN 47403
www.iuniverse.com
844-349-9409

ISBN: 978-1-6632-1396-9 (sc)
ISBN: 978-1-6632-1397-6 (e)

Library of Congress Control Number: 2021918136

Print information available on the last page.

iUniverse rev. date: 09/21/2021

LET YOUR HAPPINESS FLOW

'm gonna be happy with what I do have and continue to drink orange juice from the pulp until the oranges are abundant and the juice is flowing free. This is my philosophy.

Happiness is a state of mind. No one can make us happy or unhappy; we must establish that in ourselves. We have experiences, moments, thoughts, and feelings that are good and pure. How we interpret these things, good or bad, determines what makes us happy. The more we remember them, hold on to them, try to build on them, and take them with us, the more we re-create happiness in our minds.

Our minds are so strong that our thoughts become real to us, and even though we may find ourselves in situations that are unpleasant or unhappy, this doesn't mean we have to be. We can make the most of what we have and where we are because we control our mind. If we lead it to actions that bring happiness, it will manifest that happiness until it becomes real in our lives. So it goes from a state of mind—the same way poverty is a state of mind—to how we live.

We may be broken financially at certain times, even spend years living that way, but we don't have to accept poverty as our label. We are blessed, and though we may not feel it all the time, things change around us when we change ourselves and our ways of thinking. We have to accept this truth and put it in our minds. Eventually, we'll get to a place in life where we see it unfold, because God said He already saw us in that place in our lives—a place that makes the saying true—so it's up to us to break that block in our minds, of what society and the world show us every day and try to make us accept as reality.

Everyone's blessing is not the same. God knows just what we need, and He knows the desires of our hearts because He put them in our hearts. What may be happiness or a blessing to one person may not be the same for another person. We have to determine happiness for ourselves. That comes from praying and being real from within.

Every year, when people ask me my New Year's resolution, it's the same because it's the same one I wake up with every day—to be happy and content with who and where I am. Little do we know our resolutions don't change with the year, because the core of who we are remains the same; we just get better at being who we are and finding different approaches and avenues to reach our goals.

It's good to write goals down, but we also have to speak them into reality, saying what we believe out loud, because words bring life to the things we think about. When we say something or write it down, it's usually the first step toward making it real. While it's in our heads, it's abstract, just an idea, almost like a child waiting to be conceived. Everything that exists has been predetermined before we see it manifest in this world. Before we were conceived, it was already determined who we would be. Then our parents did the act that brought us to be, and nine months later, we were born into the world. Our goals are like our babies that haven't yet been conceived; when we write them down, we conceive our thoughts, and when we can speak them, we put them into existence.

My mom always told me to watch things I say because there's power in words. Don't put negative thoughts into the atmosphere, because that act makes them real. My mom always spoke positive things in my ear, beginning when I was a baby. She understood her part in helping to raise a child who was growing to be a man, a person in this world. The more I heard positive things about myself, it would shape who I was becoming, because if people hear something enough, they start to believe it, no matter if it's positive or negative. If you're constantly hearing that you're a loser, you're nobody, or you're not important, after a while, you begin to wear that brand—you start to live it. Words like that can cause you to fit into that role, especially if you've been hearing it since you were young, because that's the tender age of development.

On the other hand, if you hear the opposite—that you're going to be great someday, you're blessed, you're surrounded by love, and God loves you—you will begin to shape yourself to what you've been told, and you will not accept anything other than that because you've been molded and shaped to believe you are more.

I'm doing the same with my kids. I speak their greatness into existence so that as they grow, no matter what the world shows them—hardships, setbacks, disappointments, adversity, and all that comes in this life—they already have thoughts of positivity, perseverance, overcoming, and thriving because of the blessings instilled in them. They won't go far from it. We can let our children know who they are early in life, before they even reach the education system, before they go out in the world and hear what the world says about them, before they face their struggles, disappointments, and obstacles to overcome.

That's just the way it is. One of the many things that helps me through my struggles is remembering the things my mom instilled in me. When I'm going through things or even behaving in ways that *don't* match up with words she spoke in my ear when I was young, it helps me focus and remember certain behaviors that don't represent me. She'd whisper that I was going to be great, do something great someday, and do something to help somebody, so even though I may find myself in a negative situation, in a struggle, it doesn't define who I am. I shake off that negative feeling, and I get it together and begin to behave or think in a way that justifies the positive things I've been told. I know they came from a loving source.

To a large degree, we're shaped by things spoken to us, as well as our upbringing, environment, financial status, and the like. So many intangibles have an influence that ultimately who we are is determined by how we perceive and establish ourselves. It's up to the individual.

As I said, there's power in writing things down, but we also need to speak them in order to bring them from the abstract into the concrete. It starts with a simple thought—writing it down or speaking it is the vehicle that transports a thought into this world. It's the same as when parents conceive a baby: that child is predetermined; nine months later, the baby is in the world for everyone to see; and parents have an idea of the person they brought into the world because so much of who that child will be is a reflection of them. The same as when we prepare food, we know how it will taste before it reaches other people's palates because we're the ones who put in the ingredients. Our thoughts and goals are extensions of us from the creator. We're the creators of our thoughts, but the Almighty is the creator of us totally, so we have to govern our thoughts to protect our minds and be careful of the things we say. Little do we know that we affect others in the same way.

Another reason writing things down is good is because it shows us our journeys—it helps us remember where we once were in our struggles, to see our progress and growth. We grow each day. I'm not the same man I was yesterday. I'm always Brent, but today I'm Brent on this particular day, this time, this moment, and *this* right here can never be repeated or done the exact same way. When we write ourselves down, it's like a monument to refer to where we were, where we are, and how far we have come. We don't want to revisit old pains of the past to the point that it takes our minds back to relive them—no, we've been there, done that, don't need to go back. Forward is the progression we want, but we can never forget our struggles. We can never be too far removed from our pasts because things we've been through, our failures, triumphs, goals, disappointments, falling short, overcoming, and rising above, are part of who we are. And most important, other people may be in it right now, and we can help them to overcome by sharing what we've been through. So write your goals down, but don't forget your struggles. You might not get there and achieve your goals when you expected, but you will get there.

Put your goals in your heart, and make it real to you—if to no one else, just if it's real to you. The more you stay true to what's in your heart, the more you do to justify and make it real, because while you're making it real, you're re-creating happiness—what happiness is to you—and that's the energy and passion needed to fuel you. So while you may be the sole believer in yourself, don't worry about that, because sand on the beach is made up of a whole bunch of sand, and at one point, it had to start with just one grain. They grouped together with those that were the same, and the result was sand on the shore—a beach. Stay true to who you are. Belief in God will cause others who are like-minded to gravitate to one another, to pull from and give to one another. Next thing you know, you have a group of people driven by the same cause, ultimately helping one another accomplish their cause by helping individuals reach their goals.

"To thine own self be true" is what's been repeated. Write down your goals, and don't worry if they seem too far out of reach, too unrealistic, because the only limits that exist are those we acknowledge to fit us. I went in my dictionary, and I took a marker and blacked out the word *impossible* because I don't want to know what it means. God says *all* things are possible, so if God is the Almighty, my creator, and the source of all things, and my advantage is that He knows me also, then when He said what He said, He must have included me and you—He must've had us in mind too. So He tells me all things are possible with Him, and that's all I need. I don't even want to know what *impossible* means, don't want to know the definition, don't want to know that word exists—that word holds no power in my world.

"I'm in this world but not of it." We all know that from the Bible, so I can shape the world in which I live. I've learned to ignore the ignorance to which the world tries to confine me. No limits go beyond that. As far as my own li'l space in this big world, the word *impossible* can't exist, because God already said He holds all power and that all things are possible with Him. That's all I need to know. As you write down your goals, you see how far or how close you are to them, but it's a process, much like what a blueprint is in building a house. When a contractor is building a house, he gets with an architect, and the architect prints out the objective. Contractors have tools and a certification to build a house. Architects have the vision to design the house and the skills to tell contractors what they need. They then work together to manifest the vision. To manifest is so significant; to take what's in the abstract, what's in the thought process, and bring that into this world so it can be real, seen, touched, and felt—to make it happen is the key. They come together and get a blueprint.

The contractor presents the blueprint to one of his foremen. Ultimately, a buyer comes and lives in the house. It's a process, but just like a house from beginning to end, it all started with someone having a vision and believing in that vision so much that they shared it with another individual who could help them with the next part of making the vision a reality.

Therefore, we must write our goals down on paper, and we must speak positively into existence what we want our children to see as their future. We must speak positively to those around us because we never know who is listening and what messages might spark something inside of them, leading them to go and affect others in a positive way.

Never give up, and never accept your current situation as permanent; if you're not happy or satisfied in a place in your life, then that's not where you're supposed to be. I believe, though, that it's important to be grateful, to be thankful in all circumstances, because it's still a part of where you are and where you're going. Sometimes people view money or a lack of it, or fame or a lack of it, as permanent when it may only be temporary; they may see a given situation as attributable to their having good or bad luck. One of my homeboys would always say, "If it wasn't for bad luck, I wouldn't have any luck at all." Well, I don't believe in luck. Things in this world like money and fame, even luck, can be like a mirage, not real—especially the distractions and temptations that come with them. I felt the same way when my homeboy would talk about his bad luck. It ain't real; what's real is what's inside you. We hold slots in time, in life, and we're breathing them, living them, and no one can be in our slots at this time but us. This moment right here, right now, is all we have, and what we do with it is up to us. It's also up to us when we decide to make it that special moment—the one that changes and catapults us to the next level of our lives.

I'm not speaking from the standpoint of an expert or telling anyone how to think or how to live. This is my philosophy, and my actions and experiences in my life have led me to this point. I'm speaking from my point of view. I don't have all the answers, and I may not have any for you, because I'm a flawed vessel down here on this earth, living life, trying to find my way through. But I'm still here, and it's not because of luck, so my experiences, good or bad, must have had some impact on the man I am today. I feel that if it didn't destroy me, it must've made me stronger. It's what I had to go through to get here.

Everybody *done* stood on somebody's shoulders to get a better view of what's beyond the fence. We all had to stand and be lifted up on a lot of other people's shoulders to get a better glimpse where we're trying to go. We've pulled from them as they have given to us, only to pass it on to someone else. Young men have visions, older men have dreams, my visions piggyback on those before me who had dreams, and they in turn piggyback off our dreams to your visions. It helps to shape a better place for those after us. It's all the same ultimate cause. So many people have lived and died for the cause. We bring our goals and thoughts to the table, but we all are still driven by the cause, the purpose, the core of who we are.

If we *ain't* living for our purpose, then there *ain't* no purpose in our living. Have you ever felt like no matter what you do, it's pointless? Don't mean nothin', ain't gettin' nowhere? I've felt that a lot. I still feel it at times, because I'm here in this body and I'm subject to things this life throws at me. But still, it's what's inside me that gets me to the next step. If something hurts, I'm *gonna* feel the pain; that's just how the body works. You know that feeling where you go forward two steps but get thrown back three and all your energy and efforts are spent just trying to break even, trying to get out of the dungeon. Like we all started this marathon (not race) of life—because life is a marathon. We win and lose races, but a marathon is a long haul. Don't matter who finishes the race first; it's how you run.

It is much like the dash in between your start and finish—it's your story. Mine started March 26, 1978—with my birth, my marathon, my dash, started. I know it ends on the day that I die. How I fill the space between start and finish, how I run my dash, represents how I live my life while I am here. We all start this marathon in the same place, at birth, but it doesn't take long for us to see that our starts aren't as equal as we're told. Even if we've all applied ourselves the best we can to get ahead, we don't all have the same results. So yeah, it seems like we move forward two steps only to get knocked back three, but remember that many things we see in this world are like mirages. Some things in life that are not real, like mirages, serve only to confuse and distract us from what is real—from what's always inside us and what we know to be true.

A harsh reality for us to accept is that choices we make have everything to do with where we are and how big a responsibility we have. I know this firsthand. I *didn't* finish college, I had children outside marriage, and I got involved in a few things I shouldn't have, so that has a lot to do with where I am now, but it doesn't define me. We are a subtotal of choices and decisions we have made, but all subtotal means is not to stop there. Who we are is still ultimately up to us. We can explain our stories to someone, but no one can walk down those trails like us because those are our stories. I can say to my sons, "Look here, man. Don't touch that, don't do this, and stay away from that. It's detrimental to your well-being," and I can say it and show it until it puts a hole in my head, but eventually, they're gonna be grown men, their own men, and they're gonna have to make decisions for themselves. As much as I love them, I can't live their lives—they gotta do that—but because I love them, I'm gonna relay things to them from my experiences. I'm gonna sort of be a light so they can see their way, give them knowledge and wisdom based on what I have lived and learned about what worked and what didn't, explain what to do in some situations and what not to do, but at end of day, they have to decide for themselves. They must live their lives. I can show them right and wrong, but I can't tell my boys how to interpret experiences they will have. I can only trust that what I've instilled in them to be strong will help carry them the right way, in the right direction. I hope and pray they don't forget who they are and where they come from, but I can't do it for them. The love I have for my children is dwarfed by the infinite-minded love of God Almighty and the way He loves us as His children.

It's all a journey, family—OK, you're getting knocked back every time you think you're progressing, but don't sweat that. Remember where it all started, and remember your purpose. The shuffling back and forth is necessary to get you where you're going. I believe that, and I live that. I don't accept the failures that come as a result of setbacks. No failure is connected to *impossible* because, to me, that word doesn't exist, and the only reason I know that is because I know what failure feels like. I'm pretty sure you do too—we all have failed at something at one time or another. The most important thing is not to accept failure as a part of life. Just know that the only reason you're getting thrown back while you're trying to do something is because opposition is what comes with the territory of trying. If you were just being complacent or stagnant, you wouldn't be getting thrown back because you wouldn't be trying, and if you're not trying, you're not going forward. You're going *nowhere* because you are not moving. Sometimes it may seem useless to keep trying when you're getting knocked down, but any movement is better than none at all. When you're trying to get somewhere, the reality of you getting thrown back from any point of your progression means you are doing something that has caught the attention of your opposition.

To walk is to put one foot in front of the other; to stand is to hold a firm position. Mind, body, and spirit must be joined in together, on same page, for us to be totally complete. Our minds are where our thoughts come from, the birthplace, a blueprint of what and where we are in harmony with what we were and where we started. The body is the vehicle that transports, or manifests what the heart and mind have already agreed on. When the mind is free, you think freely. But it's just as important to liberate the sprit, as well as the mind, as where the spirit is will determine the kind of energy in which you operate. Our spirits are our direct links to God, an everlasting presence within us that can't be denied. When we accept this, we are acknowledging the God power within us.

Look at yourself as a seed planted in solid foundation by the sound and power of spoken word. Everything that comes in your life is going to either stunt or help your growth. The creator provides all the sunlight, water, and nutrients for the seed to grow and sustain life. The gratitude is toward life itself, to be thankful for the breath of life so that all these things are possible.

I look at my children, the money I make, my body, and my earthly possessions, and I realize that none of it is mine. God allowed these things to be, but it doesn't make or break who I am because that's determined from within. This works to our advantage, because things can be taken from us, but we never lose the desire that can bring things into our lives. I've lost a child—my firstborn son died when he was three months young—but I never lost the ability to make a child or the desire to be a father. We may be broke temporarily, but the ability to produce more is inside us, and that's what outside circumstances can never penetrate.

I've learned how important it is to know yourself, because *you're* gonna always follow *you* wherever *you* go. We can't always control circumstances, the things that happen to us, but we can always control how they affect us and how we react to them. We own that. If you've established in your mind that you're going to make it, no matter what, you gonna make it. The opposition is gonna say the opposite. The purpose of opposition is to oppose, so it goes against whatever you are trying to do. Because I am a man of African descent living in America, my opposition includes oppression, racism, poverty, white supremacy, and all the lingering effects of slavery. We're physically free, but we're still in mental and spiritual bondage. This doesn't have to be. You must be realistic about the source working against you, but liberate yourself by knowing who you are and the source that is working for you. The rules of this game ain't fair, but you even the playing field by learning the rules so that you can maneuver and find what works for you.

That may sound like a lot of double-talk, or useless words you may have heard before, but it's not. I know from experience that when you focus on the problem, that is all you can see, so you stay stuck in it and never find a remedy. Even once the problem is solved, we find or create another problem because our minds have to find a way to make a problematic life our reality. But if we shift our focus to the solution, we will always find one because we have programmed our minds to find the solution.

It's so important to never stop when you're confronted by problems, to never let the opposition stop you from doing what you have to do. Problems are just roads to be crossed on the way to your destination, and the opposition, no matter what it is, can take away what you need and give you burdens you don't need, all in attempts to stop you, but it loses all power when it comes down to who you are. That is your choice, and with that choice, everything is possible.

All people at some point in their lives gotta make choices, and we can live backward, controlled and dictated by things happening to us, thinking we have no choice, or we can live forward. We have to look at every single day as a new day, knowing that God loves us so much that He gave us the power to do anything. We must realize that we have to make a choice of what we're gonna do with it. Make the right choice because it will eventually determine who you will be. Establish right now who you are, who you want to be, what you want to do, what you live for, what wakes you up every day, what matters to you, and what's most important to you, and let everything around you unfold as a result of what you decide. I'm still unfolding.

Man, I tell you—progression is a trip! So much comes with it—change, growth ... life, it's ever growing, ever changing, and everlasting. Life goes on, it continues, and the sun is going to shine someplace every day. Everybody born gonna die someday. Life is what you make it, and as we grow and progress in life, the Almighty grows within us, we can have progression and continuously change things around us, we can change ourselves, we can extend ourselves to others around us and to those who are part of us. It's all so great through God.

As we move through life, hopefully, we surround ourselves with people who have our best interests at heart, people we consider true friends, who can reach back and open the door for others like it was opened for them. That is progression; that's how it feels when people have a common goal, a common interest.

I remember a time when the only progression and growth I could find were the dreads growing from my head. I know that may sound crazy, but it's true. It seemed that everything around me was dead—*nothing* was moving forward, no progression in my life. No matter what I did, the harder I tried, the more it seemed like I was working against myself. My dreads were the only things I saw that were growing every day. At least it felt that way. But that's when you gotta talk to yourself and encourage yourself to fight against the many issues of the world that seem to cause things to build up against you, slow you down, sometimes discourage you. It's as though it becomes human because it's like it's hoping and trying to impersonate our essence, our minds, who we really are, but remember things of this world produced by the hands and minds of humankind are temporary. Things of the spirit that have universal truths and respect the laws of nature are eternal.

Just as the ways of the world seem to build on strategies against our progress at times, we have to put up barriers to protect our minds and the things that keep us going and keep us encouraged, even if it doesn't make sense to anyone else. So at this point, my dreads still growing were like my encouragement for that day—how I was feeling and where I was. But don't get me wrong; I also felt truly blessed at this time. I had a son and one on the way and a steady, honest, but a very low-paying, never-give-a-brother-a-raise job. Things were going up—taxes, insurance, cost of living, everything except my paycheck. But even though this was happening, and the high point of my day was the thought of my dreads still growing on my head, it wasn't the worst thing happening.

I guess that's what growth does. I mean, it seemed like everything was dark and dead around me, and I just couldn't see any light. Yet light was all inside me; I just wasn't looking for it with the right lenses. Little did I know it was all a part of my journey. I was in the world, and I thought I was consumed by all of it, but it wasn't that way, because I wasn't in it as deep. Yet again, that's what the ways of the world do—what seems so bad ain't ever really that bad. When I took a step back, put on different lenses, and looked at how far I had come from where I had been, I realized it wasn't the worst, because I had been there already and seen my worst, my darkest time, and that's what growth will do to you.

This is why I strongly believe in always trying to be better, to grow as much as you can, because growth allows you to look at things from a different perspective, and change your view of what the worst could be. Until you experience or see firsthand how bad things can be in someone else's life. Progression is what we've done with the time from when things were to how things are now. It's only a gauge or a reference point for looking back at how far we've come, and hopefully it causes us to reflect with gratitude in our hearts. When you see how precious life is, you don't take things for granted.

Man, as I look over my life, I'm not even supposed to be here. Not to sound too dramatic, but I feel I've been living on borrowed time for a while. I had a strange experience when I was about nineteen, shortly after my son transitioned—I talk about it in detail later in the book—but it was kind of an awakening to truth and a vision that foretold everything I would have to go through as a result of *not* accepting this truth, but it wouldn't leave me alone, and I didn't know what it was until later in my life, after the trials and tribulations. I know I'm living by grace and mercy because it's like I have died already, like I have lived ten different lives. Second chances? Man, the things I did. I don't even deserve to have a second chance, and I've had so many, but again, I will never call it luck. "I must know what I'm doing because I'm still here"—that's what I used to say. Now I realize I'm still here because God must have me living for a greater purpose. Change gonna come. All things must change—as it was in the beginning, so shall it be in the end. The ups and downs and the struggles of life are all going to come, but seek truth, knowledge, and peace. Wisdom is defined as the ability to discern inner qualities and relationships; when you apply it to your life, along with that of others whom you respect, you gonna survive. "If I knew then what I know now"—we all have said and felt that at some point in our lives, but I know my priorities would have definitely been different.

PASSING THE TEST

We can pass the big test by listening in school, but do we listen to just pass the test, or do we listen to learn? Have we retained any of the information, and have we learned anything—meaning are we able to apply it to our daily lives? My children make the honor roll, and right now, I have more children than the number of times I've even been on the honor roll, and that's nothing to be proud of, because being on the honor roll is a great thing. But what I am proud of is that I've learned a lot about life and gained knowledge that I can pass on to my children. To me, that's what passing the test is all about. I tell them, "As long as Daddy's doing what he has to do, you have no worries. Your only job is school and self-development." Learning, excelling, and making the honor roll are what I want my children to be about right now because we are all created to reach our fullest potential and to be the best God created us to be. Receiving good grades and test scores and earning degrees and certificates are immediate rewards for the work they're going to do in school, but it's also important for them to learn about life and what it has to teach them, because all knowledge will not come from their books; a big part of it will come from just living, being aware of surroundings, and being good listeners to those who can teach them—those with wisdom. The kind of wisdom I have now don't get rewarded with a grade—no more report cards for me. The kind of evaluation that matters to me now is how I use lessons learned to give a lift up, to help others find their best way, and to help my children pass the test. I've paid, and I am still paying for what I didn't know.

Knowledge is knowing what the test is about, the ability to pass a test from what you have learned, but wisdom is knowledge to go to the next level of that class. I can have a pocketful of money, and that may put me in position to do things, but it doesn't mean I'm successful or wealthy; it just means that I have a pocketful of money at the moment. If that's all that defines somebody, then right there is as far as they'll go. I believe that to keep growing, you should ask yourself the right questions: Have I taken the necessary steps to earn the right to say I'm done? Have I paid my dues? Is there more from where that came? If not, after it runs out, do I have what it takes to get more? These are the questions I ask myself each time after I leap over an obstacle and celebrate an accomplishment, no matter how big or small. I ask, What was the source? Does someone have to come through me to get what I have, whatever it is? Do I know the way? If I know the way, can I show others how to get there or at least point them in the right direction? Can I be a light for them?

You passed the test, right? You know how to do this now. You've had some of the knocks and felt some of the success; you know some of the questions that will need answers—what they're looking for. I believe this is the way to help those who may be struggling in their lives. Those who are important in your life and maybe just people along your path may see you as a link to some of their questions, some of their answers.

Like on a test in class, surely you can tell somebody else what you know because you already passed the test, right? The same as in life, when you have made it to a certain point and experienced valuable lessons, that's like passing the test. This lends itself to the saying "Reach one, Teach one." You may not be able to guarantee him an "A", but you can help a brother by letting him know some of how you achieved your "A". You could be at the top of your game, and financially able to put money in a brother's pocket, but if you not allowing him to feed from you, to learn how you at least did it, then you ain't got nothin' but money in yo pocket, and you just tossing him a fish. In such a case, my questions would be as follows: Where did that fish come from? How did you catch it? How do I get my own? Because I can eat of just what you give me, but when it runs out, I gotta come back to you for more. And when I come back, I may have somebody with me, like a family—more mouths to feed—and they're ultimately gonna be looking to me to bring more of what I gave them. I wanna pass on what I got, plus some of what you gave me. So show me, teach me, how to do that.

There's always going to be someone behind you hungry to learn. I wanna learn. Yeah, I did good on my test, and I made it to a grown man. And yeah, I got money in my pocket. A person could be smart, even rich—yeah, that's what's up—but am I receptive and humble enough to listen and always be in a student position of learning? Success is not measured by the tangible things in your life; that's just evidence. Success is the energy, motivation, and drive that brings the things you want in your life.

A lot of people reach a certain level and forget they have money in their pockets for a reason and have reached the platform for a reason greater than themselves. They have voices that can be heard and can be a major influence over youth, sometimes more than their parents', unfortunately. But whether it's your home, your community, or something else, somebody is listening to every word you say—someone right now sees you as someone important because this person feels you've made it. I'm sure if you're reading this, you can see the face of someone who may have viewed you that way. They were looking at you. Did you stop for a moment and listen to their story? I mean *really* listen. You know they're watching, so you walk with a different strut, but it should be a walk of respect and humility because you know they're watching and waiting for any help or any advice you can give to help them pass their test as well.

If you're gonna help someone, you've gotta listen so you know where they need the help. I believe we get there to pull the ones behind us up and possibly take them farther. When you reach back to help somebody, don't look for them to make it the same exact way you did, but just by being there and starting it, you can show them by example how they can make it. They may even take a page from your life and make theirs better, but I believe they will make it if you just reach back to listen to them, hear what they say, relate to what's real to them, and help them make their orange juice.

Chastisement, punishment, and consequences are all sometimes needed and effective, but nothing is more needed and effective than just listening. On every aspect, listen to others and have the discipline to be still, to be quiet, and to listen to the inner voice and infinite wisdom of the Almighty. I struggle with this myself—I draw when I should write, I talk when I should listen, I act when I should be still—but I'm learning and still growing, and most of all, I'm listening.

I remember when my oldest son was little and used Band-Aids—he would literally go through a whole box of them to heal a wound. Eventually, the dollars started adding up just for replacing boxes of Band-Aids. (I was a single dad on a tight budget, so even replacing Band-Aids could put a dent in my pocket!) I would say, "Hey, man, what's up with so many Band-Aids?" He told me he kept putting on Band-Aids and the sticky part kept falling off, so he'd just grab another. Finally, I looked at his wound. It was a small scar to me, but to him, it was big. I guess at some point when he was smaller, he may have come to me with a little scrape, and I'd put a Band-Aid on it, and it would feel better. In his mind, it healed the wound. I relate this to his growing into a man.

When he was a small boy, he had small scrapes, and Band-Aids worked for them, but when he started growing into a man, his issues became bigger, and a Band-Aid couldn't fix those wounds. A boy grows to a man right before your eyes, and when you're a father, it seems that boys watch and listen to you more closely than girls do because they see themselves in you. It's like my boy was saying: "Pops, when I was younger, my issues were like small scrapes and could be fixed with a Band-Aid, but I'm growing with you—as you grow, I grow. I'm an extension of you. I need to be heard and taught by you now."

It's like my son, our sons, are saying: "I'm watching you, Pops. You're the first idea, first image in my mind, of how to be a man and who to be. Band-Aids don't work to fix and heal no more. Those were for when I was a little boy, but now wounds go deeper. The world was different when you were coming into your manhood, Pops, so the world is going to be different and more complex for me. I need you to really look at my wound, to really listen to me if you are going to help me, because you not listening is the same as the Band-Aid not sticking."

I see the Band-Aid as a representation of a cover for the scars that life will bring. Personally, I had to keep using them until one would stick, and in the case of my life, I needed one that would hold me where I was. After a while, they didn't work.

Do we give the same old Band-Aids to our sons that were given to us, provided there was a Pops around handing out a Band-Aid (because we realize that oftentimes the male figure is missing), or do we listen and help them deal with their unique wounds and how deep their wounds go? Do we change the bandage to fit the injury or look at their wounds as how the world has changed?

These are the questions that may be posed to us. These are questions our sons may one day ask, and when they do, will you be ready? I'm ready to answer mine. I would say, "No, son, don't follow me and do things the same way I did. Don't make the same mistakes I made to try to minimize the scar. Be better than me, and let me hold the light for you so you'll at least see where you're going. Daddy has had failures, but I'm gonna let you know those failures and put it all on the table for you because I never want anybody to tell you something about me that I didn't already tell you. The thing I do feel successful at is being a father to you. Don't follow me; follow God. He's who I'm learning to follow more and more each day. He is going to stick by you when nothing or nobody else will. I know it will make you happy, and I know I will always listen when you need to talk and be a light to help guide you. I pray this advice will lead you to a good place."

Helping your son or any young man become a man is like that—it's the reason why it's so important to listen. You don't want to have ignored all the Band-Aids he was using only to find out later that had you listened, you would have known that the wound went deeper than the Band-Aid could have reached or healed; you could have better understood his challenges in the face of his adversities.

MANHOOD (MY ADVERSITIES NOW HAND OVER OUR DESTINY)

It's hard to say you're a man when you ain't been through nothin'—if you ain't crossed over no bridges or faced no adversities—because to me, it's the adversities man faces and uses that lead him to stand tall over his and others' destiny. *Our* destiny? Yes, *ours*, because as young boys are groomed to be men, so will their learned lessons lead others to follow, so I guess the things I've been through are gonna help somebody. Is it gonna be like a show-and-tell of where we trying to go? Because the only reason we should be going back into bondage is to liberate others, not to revisit it ourselves.

JOURNEY ON

Gotta keep that special place in our hearts for the elderly, our ancestors, the ones who paved the way before us. God bless them. They are our links to our culture, our heritage, from ancient Africa to the indigenous people of this land—straight lineage to us. We need to acknowledge them and teach the youth about those who preceded us, or they won't have any joint connection to their history. I was blessed—I got to know several of my grandparents: my grandma Mary, my dad's mom, and my granddad Andrew, my mom's dad. My dad never knew his dad, as he'd died before they could meet, but we had Johnny, his stepdad. My grandma Louella, my mom's mama—I never met her either, but I feel like I knew her. My mom tells me she was a writer, a poet. She was way ahead of her time in her thinking. In fact, she wrote a poem called "Why Not a Negro for President" way back in 1945. I've learned a lot about her from my mom and from other family at our family reunions, and I feel I know my grandma now. She was really something special. Maybe she's the reason I feel at peace when I'm writing stuff.

My paternal grandma, Mary—I got to know her because I grew up around her. I remember those Cream of Wheat mornings and the fun I used to have with her. My cousin and I would finish our baths, and she would play the saxophone. She had played in high school and still remembered enough to entertain us. I remember enough good things about her to entertain my soul for years. God bless the elderly, man—they give and leave us so much. That's why whether our kids get to meet any of their elders, we have to be the ones to paint the pictures in their memories, to teach our stories, because we can't depend solely on schools.

I'm sure we all have stories to tell, but when I think about mine, my journey, my grandmas are always a big part of it because they were real women in my eyes. Strong but at the same time like beautifully fragranced flowers. I need fragrances—men thrive on them, so as men, we need pretty, soft flowers around us. Women, true women, are like flowers. Men need that soft touch. Women are like water while men are like rock, solid, but men would sink to the bottom without real women.

That's where I get my solid foundation of faith and the importance of God in my life—the strong women who had a hand in raising me. So, Lord, I'm faithful when I say I'm not ready to exit here yet. If You wanted me gone, I would have been a long time ago. I know it's possible with You. I can do all things through Christ Jesus, who strengthens me. You are the blueprint. You did it, and You put what You have, who You are, into me, so that means I can do it. I can deal with my struggles and continue this journey just because I know You love me, because if we ain't living for our purpose, then there's no purpose in living. This earth is not my home. I'm here only to do my duty as a servant, and when my work is done and I go back home, I hope I will have done a good job.

Grandparents

GOALS

---

nytime you set goals, they should always be ultimate goals of what you're trying to achieve overall. Those ultimate goals should extend beyond you, be bigger than you. You want to leave a legacy that will somehow make a change in this world—or at the least a goal to help others benefit, a goal that has your offspring in mind, way beyond them.

Any positive contribution that helps the community build up and helps the youth or anyone who feels left out, or who may not be as privileged as you, is always good. Just know it can always be worse. No matter how bad things are, there is always someone who has it worse. So even the smallest contribution to help change and reverse a cycle in which someone has been stuck is a good thing.

When we hear "great," we think of fame and recognition—we get or become known by our reputation. Being great can simply mean being the best God has created you to be, doing just what you've been called to do. Always stay humble, because roles can be switched quickly. Very few things happen overnight, but people have gone from the bottom to the top really fast—and sometimes just the opposite just as fast. I never want to look down on anyone or ever covet what another has because you never know what they had to endure, how far they had to go to get there. You may not have been made to endure as they did. Everybody's plan is different because God knows just how much each of us can handle before He sends us or allows us to go through something. What God has for someone is their blessing. It may be a big house, a fancy car, a lovely spouse, or a fabulous lifestyle, complete with expensive vacations every year— that's their blessing, and they have it. Trust that you are also blessed and may already be receiving yours in a different way. Good things come from the Lord, and when you stay on course and run your race, your blessings will come. But be mindful: your blessings may be according to your needs, and they may not be the same as another's.

When you do great things and leave behind a legacy that others can carry on, and generations after can benefit from whatever it is you have given, then you have left your mark in this world. You have left something that you hope will impact people in a positive way, and you have left them a piece of your blessings because God planted that seed in you. Remember: Your blessing may not be the big house or an extravagant lifestyle. Yours may be that you are a blessing to others, helping them achieve their greatness.

It's a known fact that many contributions have been left behind from which people benefit—everyday inventions of all kinds—but the first thing we have to recognize before we try to do anything significant is that it's not our doing. God is the ultimate one who gave us the gift to do what we're starting or doing, and He's the one who deserves all the glory. Yes, there was somebody before us who may be doing what it is we're trying to do, somebody before us who paved the way or gave us the idea and the direction, but it was God who first passed the baton. It's like a relay race. Once you've recognized your gift, once you have received your blessings, it's like He's put you in the race, and no longer is your individual performance what's most important. It's how you pass the baton to the next person.

We all have gifts; we all have something to contribute. We have something special about us. It's the same way energy works; it's continuous, it keeps going, and it was going on before we were here and will be going on long after we're gone, which is why I see us as simply vessels, like containers. If you have a cup and pour water into it, it' a cup of water; if you pour dirt into it, it's a cup of dirt—same cup but holding different things, and no matter what, it can pour out only what's been placed inside. So as vessels, we hold much within us. Whatever we surrender to ourselves has power over us, and whatever has power over us drives us. If it's greed, hatred, bitterness, lust, evil, envy—whatever it may be, whatever we fill our minds with—it will consume our minds and hearts, and that's the energy we will put out. If our minds are filled with love, positive energy, equality, strength, freedom, peace, truth, justice, and faith, then that's what we will send from us.

Being vessels means that we will be used by some higher source, because beneath the flesh and blood is spirit. When we die, our bodies wear away because they're just suits made to carry our spirits, our souls in this carnal, physical world. Underneath everything is spirit, and what has hold of our spirits is up to us as individuals—we always have a choice. We choose life over death; we choose to be used by something positive over something negative; we have choices.

God wants to bless us, and He wants us to choose His ways over the ways of the world and to spread His glory throughout. He can do it because He has all the power, but He has included us in His plan. He loves us and gave us the ability to choose. We're the only created beings who have free will to choose so many things—even the season in which we want to live, just by changing our location when it's time to do so.

Other creatures don't have a choice in this matter. God has programmed them to do what they do—lions are going to roar and hunt, and birds are going to fly, sing, and eat worms. They have instincts of danger but are not equipped to make a choice of good or evil, positive or negative, life or death. We have to choose to ask God for His will in our lives, what His plan is for us, and then ask for contentment to be at peace with His will so we can accept and embrace it with joy. This is the way I'm learning to live, to grow, and I'm learning not to worry about how I'm going to get there. I'm seeing this approach will take care of that.

I made a lot of mistakes and bad choices in my life. Everything we do in life has consequences, and I have had to deal with mine—I still am. I'm still struggling as a result of some of these decisions and consequences.

I ain't get away with nothin', and that's good, because everything we do, whether good or bad, catches up to us at some point. I still have no regrets. There are things I would do and handle differently if confronted with those same situations now, but I have no regrets because I have learned many lessons. I had children without being married, and I know that went against God's will. But everything I did and everything that happened in my life led me to where I am and the man I am now. It's also good that I didn't get away with things without consequences, because God chastises those He loves. It's like He shows us our wrongs so we have time to correct them. At least in my case, it was like He sat me down and revealed my wrongs to me, and that was the only way I was able to grow and learn.

Our conscience steps up when faced with this because we all know right from wrong, but our conscience lets us know when we reach a point where we're not listening; anytime we get to a place where we don't feel bad or remorseful about a wrong we have done, it's a sign that God's spirit is no longer with us. He has handed us over to a reprobate state of our minds, a seared conscience, and nothing can stop our lives from going in a downward spiral until we are willing to be real with ourselves and evaluate our wrongs. We can fool the whole world, but we can never fool God or ourselves.

When I was a child, my mom gave me a poem by an unknown author called "Man in the Glass." Her best friend had given it to her. I put it on my door so that it was the first thing I saw anytime I entered my room. It's about how we can go through life getting accolades—with others patting us on the back and saying "good job," the whole world loving us—but all the accomplishments from the outside mean nothing if we've failed the man or person in the glass, meaning if we can't face ourselves at the end of the day and be pleased with what we see, we have nothing.

It don't matter who's pleased with you if you ain't pleased with yourself. If you don't love yourself or realize your own self-worth, then you won't be able to receive it from anyone. Why would anyone else believe in you? There is a difference between being modest and humble and being someone with low self-confidence. So many people today, more than we realize, are using technology—social media and electronic devices—so much that it not only distracts them from humanity but also detaches them from themselves. A lot of people hide behind the things around them. They hide behind their success, their social status and friends, and their money. This total image they're trying to portray and uphold oftentimes is nothing more than the pain they're holding on to, and there are only so many things that can hide those emotions.

They allow those emotions to speak for them instead of just letting their true character be realized. I once read or heard that character is defined as the way someone thinks, feels, and behaves—a person's qualities—but that *true* character is being all the above when no one is watching. We can always show our best when we're being watched, but anytime we're being true to who we are, true to that man in the glass, we don't have to uphold a false image.

If you're being true to yourself and others don't accept you as you are, then that's a good sign that's probably someone you don't need in your life, because that person is not able to appreciate your realness. People sometimes want to place standards, restrictions, and expectations on you based on what they want, when all you should be doing is living up to standards you declare for your life.

We come into this world naked, owing no one nothin', and this world for sure don't owe us nothin'. So always be true to yourself, and don't change for anyone. I'm talking about the type of change where you no longer see yourself in the change, meaning don't change so much to please others that you no longer recognize who you are, what you believe, how you were taught, who you worship, and the morals and standards that make up a lot of who you really are, because that's the man in the glass. While a person may be happy with the changes you've made for them, happy that you've changed to become just who they want you to be, you won't be happy, because it's not in your heart.

On the other hand, sometimes you may need to make a change—for *you*—to a certain behavior of yours or even a characteristic about yourself. Certain changes like these may be needed so that you become a better you. I'm sure we all have been in this position at one time or other. I sure have. I had a dire need to make a change about myself *for myself*—I had to stop using cocaine. It was a behavior that was not me; it wasn't representative of what I believed. I knew I couldn't be the best father while I was on that. I changed for my son, but I came to this change on my own. I had to be true to myself and look at that man in the glass every day. So yes, while it was for my son, it was also for me, which is why I made the decision to change the behavior on my own. People around me could've talked a hole in my head, but until I was ready to change, it wasn't going to happen.

The important takeaway from what I'm saying is not that I was stubborn in using cocaine until I wanted to stop—no, what's important is that I was man enough, believed in myself enough, to know that using drugs was not a behavior I wanted to be known for, or for my son to know of me. I had to be true to myself and face the man in the glass and walk myself into a place to get help to change that behavior. But I'm only speaking for myself. What works for me may not work for you, so you have to do what's true to your heart, and it will lead you right.

RELATIONSHIPS

I f you're with someone and you're always happy but they're not, or they're always happy but you're not—if y'all are rarely happy together about similar things—it usually means y'all are not happy together. Y'all don't have much to share with each other. In my view, a relationship with someone in any form—whether it's love, a friendship, a business relationship, or any other kind of relationship—should be one in which the two people are enhancing each other's life in some way, helping each other grow. Some people find chaos to be the only form of order they know. To each their own, but that don't work for me. Everyone should do what works for them. Chaos is not of the Lord, and I personally like peace and harmony, so I stick with it, but again, I'm only a man speaking from my point of view.

Relationships of any kind should be some kind of service— giving and receiving. The most important relationship is the one between you and your creator. The creator, our Father, is spirit, and life is in the spirit. Freedom, justice, equality, truth, and peace are all of the spirit. The spirit is eternal, the physical is temporary, and we have physical bodies to manifest spiritual things while living in a physical world. Since our Father is the one who put us here, He is the only one who has the power to judge whether our spirits will elevate to a higher level of conscious reality or stagnate at some level or, even worse, descend to a lower dimension. So it makes sense to me to render our services to the reason we were created, and that is to glorify and praise our Father. His word, law, and judgment are what keeps the entire universe in order. He is the only one who has that right; He's the first and the last. I don't say *He* in any biased way. *He* and *she* are terms recognized only in the physical world, because the spirit has no gender. When we realize who the creator is, when we realize we are made in His image and likeness—meaning we are His reflection, made by Him for Him, not for ourselves— that's when we become masters of ourselves. We must first submit the right given to us. That is the first step and lesson on service and relationships at any level, and for any relationship that has service from only one side, and not reciprocity, the process is in bondage. But the Father is freedom because He first freed us from ourselves; we don't need to submit to any person, place, thing, idea, or group of people, or anything created, because those things don't have the power to liberate us.

Any man or woman who can embrace the truth is king or queen of his or her domain. "I said, 'You are gods; you are all sons of the Most High'" (Psalm 82:6). This birthright has been given to us as heirs to the king of creations, of God Almighty.

So when my physical body fades away and expires, as it is guaranteed to do someday, it will receive a new body to house my spirit to survive, wherever it is. I live to be with the spirit of the living God for eternity.

My purpose here is not to try to persuade anyone's belief system or say any one is dominant over another. I'm just emphasizing the importance of relationships. Oneness, unity, and relationships have been severed and divided by different races and different religions— over here, over there—saying, "We're right, and they're wrong," when in actuality there is only one race, the human race, and two religions, people who are for God and people who are not.

A relationship is a union between two people. Since people inherited the earth, the condition of the world reflects the relationships among the people here. The turmoil in the world is the result of how we are treating one another, so we need to go back and restructure our ideas regarding relationships. We need to realize who we are. It might make a difference in the way we treat the next person. There are gonna be struggles with family, but let them be struggles you can call your own. What you learn from those struggles will be what you know for yourself, not what you've been told to expect by others. Personally, I know God has loved me through all my struggles, has guided and protected me. Later, I learned a better term for struggles—it's called trials and tribulations.

I'm thankful for all mine because they prepared me and made me the man I am today.

ALIMAYU, JUNE 3, 1998

She called me from the hospital having complications. It was a concern, but it was not the first time. She was pregnant with our first child, and she'd started having complications around her fourth month. But this time, they said the baby was coming, and they were going to have to induce labor. I was all of nineteen years old, still enrolled in college, and she was only seven months pregnant. They resigned her to the hospital bed, where she was in labor for a week. I was by her side the whole time. I became her bedside nurse, changing her stool pan and everything. The actual delivery was quick, maybe only twenty minutes.

Witnessing an actual childbirth is a miracle beyond words. It's amazing to be a part of something so beautiful while knowing it's a part of you—to actually see God's work—and at only nineteen years old, I knew it was a moment in time I would never forget. He was born three pounds, two ounces, with the umbilical cord wrapped around his neck, and he was not crying. This was all new to me, so I didn't know what to make of it all. I had never seen a baby being born, so needless to say, I was confused. I thought it was normal, plus the nurses and doctors were calm, so I figured it had been a normal procedure. All I knew was I was on a euphoric high. I was feeling something that could not be matched—no drug had ever given me this feeling, and no feat I ever accomplished on the football field had either. This was something altogether different. This was a child being born—*my child*. Wow!

They cut the umbilical cord and cleaned him off, and he finally cried, li'l' fella with lungs just as small as he was, all three pounds of him, but he had ten fingers and ten toes, so all was good. They put him in an incubator, and I remember that whole night—the buzz of excitement I felt and all the hope I had of being a great father to this boy. We named him a junior and gave him the middle name Alimayu, which is African for "God is honored."

He had to stay in the hospital until he weighed more, but no worries—his mother lived right down the street from the hospital, so I stayed there during the time I was home from school. We visited every single day, read to him, held him, and talked to him, and he started to fill our whole lives. Day by day, he was getting bigger and healthier, but it was time for me to go back to school, so I kissed my girl and baby goodbye. It was tough—I didn't want to leave. The hospital released him after he was two months old, so things were getting better for my li'l' man. I felt a little more at ease, and I was feeling good about my new family, although my mom and dad were still working on their issues, and that was always on my mind.

For you to better understand how I got here, maybe I should rewind.

At a very young age, I felt what a broken home was like, as my mom and dad were divorced. My mom and I left South Florida to go up the state to Tallahassee. She never told me what was really happening. She was something else, though. The whole time we were living in another city, I never saw her with another man. Not saying there weren't any—just saying I never had to be confused by having to interact with another man, because they were never around me.

It was different in Tallahassee, and we started to like living there, but that would soon change, because when I turned seven, we packed up everything, rented a truck, got on the road, and moved back with my dad. I guess they agreed things would be different. I think my mom felt I needed to be raised with my dad, where things were supposed to be better, but after a while, they didn't feel that way. My dad was a good provider, and my mother also worked, so we lived well, traveled, lived in a nice house in a nice neighborhood, had nice cars—did all kinds of good, fun stuff families do—so it didn't seem like anything was wrong, with the exception of the few disagreements I would hear. I was never told that anything was going to change. Remember I was a kid and my mom felt that a child should not have to deal with adult problems. I guess most parents feel the same way—at least the good ones do. So while they were dealing with their issues, I was busy being a kid. With everything that was going on, all I knew was I saw my dad as strong. I loved him—he was my dad—but even so, things just weren't always cool, and I came to see this throughout my high school years.

As planned, I left for college, full of hope and ambition. My parents had saved for my college through a prepaid college fund—my mom had kept it up for years—so I had no choice; they were determined I was going to college. My parents wanted to be sure I had every opportunity to get a college education in case there were no scholarships. Although several universities made offers for me to play football, there should have been more—after all, the team I played on made history, and I'd been one of the top players. We were the first team in that school's history to have an undefeated regular season. Every one of the guys I played next to should have gotten a full ride to a Division I school, but there was more behind that game than people really knew.

Most of the schools that offered a scholarship were very far away and in super cold weather—and I hate cold weather. A university in Kalamazoo, Michigan, offered me a football scholarship. Michigan: twenty hours and about 1,500 miles away from home, with average winter temperatures practically in the single digits—*aaagh*! Not for me. So I went to my first choice, Florida A&M University in Tallahassee, a school with a historically strong black tradition and a lot of pride. I knew when I got there I wanted to play football, but I had no idea what my major was going to be because I had no idea what I wanted to do in life.

MISTAKES TO GROW BY

When I first got to school, I ran into a great group of guys. We clicked immediately—two from my hometown, the other two from other cities in Florida. They were a good set of friends, and we all had plans to graduate from college. We all liked football—except me; I *loved* football! We all tried out for the team, but we didn't make it. Honestly, I went up there mostly to play football, the game I loved. Yeah, I wanted a degree too, but school didn't mean the same to me without football. I forgot my real purpose for going to school, which was to earn a degree. First mistake.

I was living off campus in a small apartment across from a little chicken shack. Without football, there was a void in my life, so I wasn't the best person to be around. Along with my disappointment of not playing ball, I was also worried about home. My mom and dad were still dealing with some issues, but Mom was teaching, and I think that fulfilled her somewhat. Still, I didn't like her having to deal with stressful situations. It's funny how when children leave home, fathers tend to feel their jobs are done, while mothers know their jobs have just begun.

I started to lose focus in school, and my grades suffered. There

I was, failing college and not playing football. It didn't feel good. But I did know that drugs and alcohol made me feel good. Second mistake.

I felt a void that I could not explain. I thought drugs and alcohol could fill it, but they could not—they only masked whatever it was. I learned later in life that just about anything we can think to do cannot fill an existing void, because that void will only be filled by the one who made us.

Just think about that for a minute.

Back to my little family. There I was, nineteen years old, away at college, with a newborn baby and my girl at home, and though I loved them both, it was all another distraction from my studies. I was still going to classes because I really wanted to graduate, but now, with a family of my own, I had money on my mind. My mom was still teaching, but now living with her oldest sister, and my pops had his struggles he was trying to handle—but he was just a man, and struggles can get to the best of us. I know struggles.

I didn't want to ask my mom for money, because she's just a love machine. That lady will give to loved ones until there's nothing more to give. I had a little job, but it wasn't enough. So I saw where I was, on a college campus, and remembered what I knew and from where I came—the streets of Miami—so I put the two together, and ... you already know the rest. Third mistake.

I was always thinking about my baby and my girl at home. Hoping they were OK, wishing I could be there with them. So she planned a trip to bring my li'l' fella up for me to see him. He was doing well—getting healthier, getting stronger. Man! I was so happy and could not wait to show them both off to everyone. She and her sister drove up.

So my lady brought our son to my place, and I was just getting in from work, with books, food, and other things in book bag. Before they came, my place had been where people came and went from sunup to sundown. I had turned my place into a place where people came to buy weed, but I demanded respect the entire time my girl and baby were there. That's the game, so my li'l' place was cleaned up, free of smoke, quiet, and peaceful the whole weekend while they visited. It felt good to have them there. They looked good, and it was a good visit, but the weekend was short and over too soon, so I said goodbye to my girl and gave my little baby a kiss. They went back. They called and let me know they'd arrived home safely, and I went to sleep still happy and thinking how their visit had given me enough to last till the next time.

The next day, early in the morning, I got a call from someone saying the baby was not breathing. I didn't know what to do. I just wanted to get there. Before I could get the words "Take him back to the hospital" out of my mouth, her brother had scooped him up and done a full sprint to the hospital—remember it was right down the road from her house. Still, the next call I got felt like it had been days instead of just a few hours, because the next call I got, the next words I heard were …"He is dead." I felt dead.

Now I had to get my head right to go back home and bury my son. The scene was nothing for which I could have ever prepared. My dad was there. My girl was on the floor weeping. I was trying to stay strong and hold her and the other mothers up. It seemed that I was coping all right for a while, but it all came down on me at the funeral. Seeing that tiny little casket, seeing his name next to my name in the obituary—man! I had no words to describe it all.

My aunt Fran, my mom's oldest sister, was overseeing the

obituary and wanted to know if I wanted to write something. I couldn't get my mind wrapped around that—my son's obituary. How could I write a eulogy, a testimonial, a tribute to my baby boy's short three months here? But one of those late nights before the funeral, I wrote these words:

> My li'l' baby, Daddy's not too good with this. I'd
> rather tell
> U face 2 face—since your body went from warm
> to cold, so many times I wish I was in your place,
> but if I was, I would've never been your daddy.
> I'm wondering why this happened but at the same
> time still not understanding what good things I
> have done in my life to deserve to be your daddy.
>
> I'm 'bout to take a short intermission from
> writing these words. Thought I heard
> you cryin', tryin' to get my attention—must
> want to sleep on Daddy's chest again.
> Come on, baby; rest on Daddy's chest.
> That's where
> U belong forever, in that U like the
> active muscle behind my left breast.
> Think that's how we communicated—
> still infatuated by the way
> U sucked my nose, the life that
> you put inside lifeless clothes.
> U even have one of daddy's toes.

Li'l' man, this wasn't part of
our plan. Move on, I know
we can—don't worry 'bout Mama.
Me and U got her, and both
grandmas and grandpas.

'Cause Daddy know
what U prefer—anybody wit'
knowledge know once you're
born, you never die; you're
just part of everything alive.

My li'l' baby, if anyone
feels these words I'm
writin', they still don't have
a clue how much Daddy
loves you, but Daddy's not too
good with this. I'd rather tell
U face 2 face.

To Baby Brent from Daddy Brent, September 8, 1998

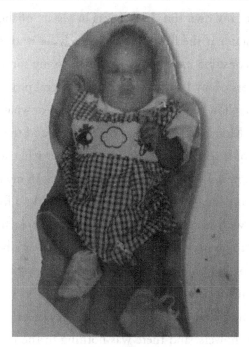

Baby Alimayu

Every week, I would get word from home, "Hey, man, another homeboy got shot up," another one gone, but this time it wasn't about somebody getting shot up, wasn't just one of my homies, someone gone forever. This time, it was my son, my only son, the one I helped nurse back to health, my baby boy. This was much harder to stomach.

At the funeral, I tried to be strong, but I just didn't feel my legs anymore. Paramedics were called afterward, and I was later told that they'd immediately noted signs that I was about to go into cardiac arrest. I finally broke. It was real. I'd lost a part of me I'd never have again, but I was still breathing. So life still was going on, but then I realized there was an emptiness inside me that couldn't be filled by anything or anyone outside myself. I had gone into brain overload at the sight of my own son dead. I was in a state of shock, almost a comatose state, at the funeral. I completely let it all go and just let the pain consume me. I did not make it to my son's burial site. Some members of my family followed the funeral procession while others had to follow the ambulance carrying me, or what felt like my lifeless body. Mom was with me at the hospital and the entire time whispered words in my ear. I cannot remember what she said, but next thing I knew, I was sitting upright and I was in my right mind, but much of my life, my journey after that, was like a fog.

I stayed with my girl as we tried to comfort each other, but finally I had to go back up the road to school. I was a broken man, and I was broken financially as well, but it's funny how when you have less, you learn to be creative. Ha ha, money was short and groceries even shorter; many times, electricity was off, I had to get used to cold showers, and there was nothing in the fridge but old tomato paste, peanut butter, and a lot of flour.

Again, I didn't want to burden my mother with anything, so I didn't let her know what was going on. I learned about peanut butter and jelly in microwave, peanut butter cookies, and pizza—all from scratch, with a little water in the mix. I was still taking classes, but I was also getting into a lot of fights. When my baby's mom came back up to see me, I was kind of heavyhearted, bullheaded, and hardened by the immediate change of events in my life. I wasn't the same young man she'd known; I was filled with anger. She was a sweet person—very loving and tried hard for us—but eventually we parted ways. There were no hard feelings between us. She was the mother of my first child, and that will always be special to me. Last I heard, she was doing really well, and I wish her the best always. Me? Well, I became the new face to an old game called cocaine—fourth mistake!

I was birthed through my mother, peace, and love, but even that wasn't enough to equip me for the battle-filled arena I was stepping into—one full of conflict, confrontation, and a bloodline that separated east from west. "The greater warrior is the one who conquers himself"—I believe in that quote. I would eventually have to make a choice. I would have to confront myself and the battle brewing within or lose myself in a cold world that was getting more chaotic.

I didn't even like to fight. I like to be at peace with people, and when I fought, I got angry—instead of the opposite, as most people get angry and *then* fight. When I was a child, I would cry when I fought, though not out of fear—I was never fearful of anything. I was just angry for allowing anyone to push me to that point, because when I made up my mind I was going to fight, it was no play-play—you're my enemy at that moment, and we're fighting till somebody falls.

I would rather die before I let anyone push me around or have their way with me, and I was so adamant about this that when I was in my teens, I put a permanent mark on my arm to remind me of this pledge as I went through life. I'm not saying this is cool or anything. What I'm saying is always be true to yourself. Don't accept anything that belittles you, and always remind yourself that you count, that you matter.

This is why I'm so thankful every day for God being in life, because as a young man, I was angry and didn't always control my anger, but I never wanted to hurt anybody, and I never did, and that's why I'm so thankful to God, because He is the only one I feared.

As I got older and all through my teenage years, the only other thing I was afraid of was my mom's wrath (ha ha). I was more concerned about disappointing her than about receiving an actual beating, which, from her or my dad, was rare. I didn't want to get that li'l' lady upset. If I do wrong, I get out of jail when my time is up; I can dodge a bullet if it's not my time; I can deal with people of all kinds—but when it came to my mom, I had to live under the same roof, and I never wanted to face her when I did anything wrong.

As I said, it wasn't that I got beatings. In fact, if I count the number of times my mom may have turned her wrath on me physically, I wouldn't even use half my fingers, so that wasn't my concern for messing up. It was hurting or displeasing her in any way. I guess that's what the Bible calls honoring your mother and father. I truly respect that commandment.

I didn't grow up with siblings, but I had my cousins, thank God. Everywhere my cousins went, I was always with them; I was li'l' cous' following them around. I'm also thankful for my two sisters—we all have the same dad, but we grew up in separate households. We're all close, and I love both very much. Still, in my household, there was only me, and that was not easy. But as I said, I had my cousins. They were my brothers. "Where y'all going?"—I was always ready to hang with them. They'd say, "Shut up, li'l' dude, and just come on, Guy." Ha ha. That's the name my uncle gave me, Guy, when I was a li'l' squat. He would always say, "Hey, y'all know he's just a guy," so it stuck with me in my family. Some of them still call me Guy to this day. In fact, my two-year-old son's middle name is Guy. It's kind of a tribute to my uncle, the same one who gave me that nickname.

When I think about it, my uncle's life and my life kind of

paralleled in some ways. We both lost our sons. His son was tragically gunned down at about fourteen years old. My cous' was leaving from a teenage joint with a few friends, and some dudes from the other side of town followed them and shot my cous' down, killed him. That was a tough one because everybody loved him and he looked just like his dad, my uncle.

My uncle was a special man and one of my favorites. He and my dad were close, and my dad trusted him—I could tell. One day, my dad asked him to come over and be at the house because we were treating the house for termites and had just put a tent on the house. My mom was coming back from a weeklong school trip, and my dad was going to be working late, so he needed someone in the house with us while the men were going to be there cleaning up. My dad was protective like that. Later, my mom left for food, so it was just me and my uncle at home. He was in the backyard doing his thing—that's how he was, sort of a loner, never bothered anybody for anything. My mom was crazy about him, and he was a real character, very funny and entertaining as hell. He was one of a kind. I didn't know anybody who didn't like this dude or who ever said anything bad about him. He was just one of those lovable kinds of people.

I was in my room playing video games or talking to some female on the phone. Later, my mom got back and asked if I knew where my uncle was. I was like, "He was out back last time I checked. Maybe he went to the store or someplace." We waited and waited, thinking that's what he'd done, even though he didn't really know our neighborhood. It got dark, and still he wasn't back, and by this time, my dad was home. He started getting worried—we all did—so he decided to report my uncle as missing.

They searched everywhere in the neighborhood, and then finally they searched the water. My uncle wasn't missing anymore. They found him in the lake behind our house. My uncle was dead. He had drowned.

I remember I used to follow my uncle around my grandma's neighborhood when I was a li'l' dude. He would go to the housing projects to hang out and cut hair. I should have been hanging out with him out back that day, just kickin' the breeze, chillin', talkin' with him, and listening to him like I used to do, but I wasn't. And I can remember feeling so guilty about that, because I hadn't been back there to save him.

He must have tried to look in the water, gotten too close, and slipped. I blamed myself for a long time because I thought if I had been there with him, I might have seen him stumble in the water and pulled him out. I don't know, man—when you're fourteen years old, you think you're invincible, too much Superman, I guess. (And there's that parallel again: he lost his fourteen-year-old son, and I was fourteen when I lost him.) But I felt I would've been able to save him, as I'm a really good swimmer, thanks to my dad.

That was my uncle, my pops's li'l' brother—and he loved him, always looked out and took responsibility for him. That's what I teach my sons, to always look out for one another. I tell them, "Y'all are each other's responsibility. Y'all are brothers."

Uncle drowned that night out back, but I think he really died two years before, when his son was killed. I hadn't been out there to save him, but I forgave myself finally because I realized that we can't beat ourselves up while we forgive others. Life goes on, and as hard as it was, I had to accept that he was gone. That was Uncle Pee-Wee. Rest in peace, Unc. I know I'll see you again. I'm just so thankful that you played such a role in my journey.

Growing up with my cousins was something else. I was the youngest in the group. We looked out for one another, we had loyalty to family, and sticking together was never under debate, because oftentimes, family is all we got. When one of us ate, we all ate. That was our grandma and granddad's rule, and by the same token, if one of us got a whipping, we all got one. But all in all, we had big fun growing up. We played football and a lot of street ball. It was always one neighborhood against another, or one street against the other, but it was all in fun. We even sprayed marks on some streets to make it look like a real football field. I don't see children doing things like that much anymore—they hardly go out to play, so many electronic devices. But we were always outside, and we were never bored. We were creative.

We always stayed in mischief of some kind, but that was to be expected, as we were young boys growing up in the streets of Miami. We knew our neighborhood. Some areas were worse than others, and Liberty City, where we were, was one of them. I remember my great-grandma's backyard seemed like a whole neighborhood of its own—it seemed so big when I was young, like we had room to run for days back there. Every day was like an adventure, always something new to do. Man, those were some good days, and you might have found us anywhere because we knew our way around. I was mostly following my cousins, going wherever they went, doing whatever they did. We saw a lot, heard a lot, and learned a lot. I feel that made us grow up fast. I know it helped me become the man I am today.

I learned about survival, improvisation, and humility; how to deal with my fears and not be afraid of anyone or anything; how to stand on my own two feet and hold my ground, no matter the environment; how to fight; how to say the right things to a girl; and how to hold my own—all from growing up in Miami and rolling around with my cousins. We got older and paved our own paths in life, but we are always family, and they have always been there for me, right by my side, when I needed them most, just as I have for them. We are still that way to this day. So I'm thankful for my cousins during that part of my journey. A lot of other family, like my grandmas, aunts, and uncles, all played a big part in helping my parents raise me, but my mom was major.

When you see guys on the big screen always saying "Hi, mom" when the cameras hit them, it's not that they're taking away from their dads; it's just that, most times, moms are the ones who are always there. A lot of men don't even know their dads, though that was not the case for me. Unlike some of my cousins' fathers, my dad was in the home, and that was good in a lot of ways yet also confusing. The thing is—a dad can be there physically but not really be in touch. I've never been a person who makes excuses—I believe in owning up to my mistakes in life, manning up to the steps I took toward manhood, good or bad, right or wrong—but I also believe that when a boy starts moving into manhood, he needs the guidance of someone who knows what it's all about, what becoming a man is all about, because they've been where you're going. If you're fortunate enough to have a dad, he's usually the one to do that. Whether he's in the home, it's the quality time spent in teaching his son skills about life, mostly things about his life and sharing experiences he's had—good ones, bad ones, the ones he came through, the ones he didn't. As a young man, you have to take some bumps and bruises on your own and be able to get up from them and learn from them, so I'm not saying having a dad protects you from that, but having one should mean you have someone who holds the light so you can at least see where you're going.

Being close enough to your son so that he sees you as his best friend above all his friends—that's the biggest gift a dad can give to his son. When he can talk to him about anything and everything and he's not judged by him, that's priceless. I use every incident my sons deal with in their young lives as a teachable moment, a lesson on how to handle a situation if it comes again. If they're angry with one another, fighting one another, feeling low about themselves or even a li'l' too full of themselves, I try to teach them how to handle it better.

I'm in their lives, not just around them, and although they don't all live with me, the time I spend is quality time; whenever I'm with them, I make it count. When a man *don't* take time to just do that, then I think he done already lost something he can never get back. My sons ages are ages two through eleven, so when they get older, they're gonna be all right coming to me to talk about stuff going on in their lives, from feelings about girls to questions about drugs or anything else.

LEARNING WHO I AM

first tried cocaine to see what made it so powerful; it's taken men away from their families and ruined their careers. After I tried it, I didn't see the big deal. Like I said, I don't make excuses for my bumps, but I kept trying to get high from it until it became a heavy habit. I was trying to see if it was strong enough to pull me away from what was important to me. But it never did, thank God— nothing in my life ever had that strong a hold on me. There was never such a strong hold that it completely caught me up, where I was doomed and couldn't get back up. It was like I would let myself go way out deep in the middle of the ocean, but God always had His hand on me and kept me in His grip. I felt that whenever He would see me drifting too far, He would pull me back.

It became a strong habit, but it never had a hold on me. The whole time, it was never something I enjoyed doing, but by the time I realized what I was doing, I was grown. During so many pivotal times in my life, I had lots of questions, a lot of things I just wanted to talk to about, but I had to find answers on my own. I did have a rebellious attitude and really wasn't trying to hear nothing nobody was saying. I never disrespected anything my dad would say—it's just that, during that time, not much was being said by him. It was a weird feeling, a distant feeling, but he was my dad, and I knew he loved me. It's just that somehow it was kind of confusing to me at times, but from the outside, people thought I had it made, and it wasn't really like that.

Dads need to really understand the importance of the quality time they spend with their kids. You can have the most important job in the world, making good money, but when a kid is young, that money doesn't have the same value to the child that it has to you. You could be married to the child's mom or not, because some of the best father-son relationships happen, also, when the father and mother are not married. You can do things as a family at times—going to football games and being your son's biggest fan are important—but if you're not putting in the quality time with him, teaching him and allowing him to pick your brain just to see if he's thinking right, just to let him stand behind your shadow sometimes for his justified measurement, then you have missed an important part.

My dad worked smart, and he worked hard. He provided for us very well because all he wanted to do was give his family better than what he had had. He'd never known his dad, so he'd had no pattern to follow. Wanting better for your family is what every man should want. It's definitely what my dad wanted. I know my pops's heart was in the right place—to be the father he didn't have. It's just that as I grew older, so did his business, until it seemed he wasn't around much. Like Grandma would tell me, "He means well."

For the longest time, I didn't want to get married, because my only memory of marriage was failure. I had seen it at home and with other family members. So no wonder, to me, marriage meant arguments, bad feelings, sacrifice with little rewards, and sometimes emptiness. I loved the holidays, as it would be like one big happy family for a short while, but afterward, it would start all over until the end of the year rolled around. I'm sure so many of us can relate to that.

Don't get me wrong—I didn't have a bad childhood. My dad wanted the best for us, as I've already said, and we took trips, lived well, and often would have cookouts with friends and family. We even had season tickets for the Miami Dolphins games; I met famous people with my dad. So I'm thankful for many things, but even with all the good, I remember some very confusing years growing up.

Moms have a way of making things look better than they really are—mine did. I had no idea how things really were, and much of that was because she worked so hard trying to keep the family together, as I'm sure many mothers do. They make it right, like my mom did. She was the glue that held it all together. I know that wasn't easy, but she took the role of a mother serious regardless of what she was dealing with. When I look back on the time when it was just the two of us, I realize it's like the sacrifices she made were necessary because she knew she was now responsible for raising a man. She knew that I would be watching everything she was doing, and she understood how important the image of my dad was to me. As I said before, I never saw another man around; she knew a father's image to a young man should be cherished, no matter what the relationship was like between the parents. It's important to uphold the image that a young man sees when he looks in the mirror. Boys look up to their fathers and notice how their moms and others respect them. I really wish more young mothers today would adopt that same mentality and really understand what it means to be a mother. It should be an honor and a privilege to bring a life into this world.

Both my mom and my dad gave me their best, and I'm thankful, but I was lonely and timid at times because I just didn't know how to really enjoy myself and be happy. I never knew when something would change the mood. There were times when we would go out to dinner—this was after I was older—and I could feel the tension. I guess that's normal in any marriage, but we would be all smiles through it all. When I look back now, I realize that's what decent parents do—they protect their children from all the issues and problems.

I love my dad and understand the past. I truly have forgiveness for him in my heart because of that love. I realized I had to live my life and understand people. We are all human, and people sometimes forget that dads are just humans too, although to children they seem bigger than life. I learned to understand that it can always be worse, and some of us have seen worst, but we keep going because we know that nothing is worse than being without your dad or never knowing him.

My joy doesn't change, but it was always me and my mom. "You and me against the world" was what we used to say because it described us, as so many times we were all we had. Sometimes money was limited with only one paycheck, but my mom knew we were not alone. We always had family to fall on if necessary, but my mom believed in being independent. She never got help from the government or went to the courts for to demand any support, so most times, it was just us.

This was especially true when we lived in Tallahassee a few years, when I was about six years old. Mom was a part of everything I did, from taking me to T-ball practice (no Little League football in Tallahassee—that came later), birthday parties, and other events to helping me with my schoolwork and even keeping up with my friends. We got such a strong bond because she has always been my biggest supporter. She invested so much time and always believed in me. Through so many struggles and hardships of my life, it was my mother's love and prayers that pulled me through. She never, ever gave up on me. Before we moved to Tallahassee, when she was still trying to make our family work, I remember a lot of Fridays getting picked up after school with the car packed, and we would hit the road, get away. Most times, we would go to Orlando, get a hotel, and spend a weekend at Disney World. I was young, so it was all fun to me, but not for Mom. She was getting me away so that we wouldn't have a sorry weekend around the house. She would never tarnish my father's image in my eyes, because she wanted me to grow and form my own opinion of things, not use her experiences as my measuring tool. She felt that children should have fun and be happy, not have their minds occupied with things they didn't understand.

That's loving your child, because no matter what's going on, a child loves both parents, and no one has the right to kill that child's joy. Couples today should learn that. No parent should ever say negative words to their children about the other. My mother never spoke negatively to me about my dad—nor he about her, not ever.

I loved being with my dad. He taught me to swim and answered all my crazy little-kid questions, and we played boxing with real boxing gloves my mom got us one Christmas. I didn't know it then, but he was teaching me how to defend myself. Ha ha, it was funny because he would get on his knees to be eye level with me, and sometimes I would get in some real hard punches. It was all in fun, though. He also wanted me to experience some of the finer places to dine so that I would know the best and want the best. Through these years, or what seemed like the happy times while they were still married, my mom still never told me anything was wrong. She let me get to know certain things about our family's struggles on my own. Eventually, the time would come when I would see things more clearly and understand the reason for all our road trips.

All the things my mom had gone through, and I never saw her cry. But I do remember once during my angry years, when I was mad at the world, I said some harsh words to her. When she cried, I hugged her and told her I was sorry, and I never, ever spoke to my mom like that again. I never had before that—it was just one of those frustrating times of my life.

My mom displayed so much strength—still does—and has always been a strong person, but one particular road trip, she had had enough. She picked me up, and I don't even know whether it was a Friday, and that's how we came to live in Tallahassee. Mom said that this time we were hitting the road for good.

My mom had a college friend who lived there. She and my mom were like sisters, and as far as we kids were concerned, we were all family, so my mom was Aunt to her kids, and she was Aunt to me. She was a single mom, had two kids, but her daughter was older, so like my mom, she was raising a son. We were always at each other's place. Those were some real happy times for all of us. Tallahassee was a good place, my kind of town—quiet, laid-back, country, old-fashioned, and simple. We loved it up there. We had a few rough times getting adjusted, but we managed. I had a group of friends I clicked with, and I started to really get used to Tallahassee. My mom and I still talk about Tallahassee and joke about how we should have stayed. Of course, we missed home, because, to me, there wasn't any place on earth like Miami.

My mom and dad were already separated before we decided to make Tallahassee our home, so I didn't understand it all. Why did we still have to move away? It was kind of unsettling to me because, to a child, any move is a lot, but the biggest thing to a child, no matter where they live, is about clicking with their friends.

Howard, a small subdivision in South Miami, is where I first lived with my mom and dad. After my parents' separation, Mom and I lived in several places in the Miami area. That's when it seemed like we moved a lot. Actually, we lived in only three different neighborhoods before leaving South Florida, but through a child's eyes, it seemed it was almost every neighborhood in Miami. We lived in Carol City, another residential area near Carol City, and finally Hialeah. We stayed the longest in Carol City.

We lived in these places when I was young, and even though I was only six years old, I remember something special about each one of them. Still, to this day, my favorite was with my aunt in Carol City.

I loved that li'l' neighborhood. I knew everyone, and they all knew me. My mom worked, so my aunt used to pick me up from school and would have a peanut-butter-and-jelly sandwich ready, along with my favorite cartoon showing, and then I would go out to play. Good people, good memories.

The other neighborhood that sticks out is the one in which our house's kitchen caught on fire. My cousin and I were outside playing when he noticed smoke coming from the house. It was our house, and my mom was inside. She had just put a new bolt lock on the front door because she wanted to protect us, but there was a key for it, and my mom panicked and couldn't find it. So she was locked in, trying to put the fire out before the fire department got there.

It was a bad fire, but it didn't burn the whole kitchen—just an area above and around the stove. The worst of it was to my mom. It was a grease fire, as she'd been frying fish. The stove was faulty and didn't regulate the heat right, so the burner may have shown medium, but the heat it was generating was high. My mom panicked and made the mistake of throwing water on it, which made the fire more aggressive. She was burned really badly all up her arm, and the scar is still there today. Thankfully, by the grace of God, she was unscathed except for her arm. We weren't there long either. We moved after the fire because she didn't feel safe living there.

My mom protected me, and in my eyes, she was like a superhero. I remember we had an old car during this time that we named the Green Hornet—that made it fun, because it was always breaking down. Thankfully, someone would always come along and help us get it rolling again, and my mom never showed how frustrated she was, when she really could have. All she cared about was getting me to school and getting herself to work. I later realized that those times I would get out the car to stand near my mom whenever someone (usually a man) stopped to help with the Green Hornet, or the times I would check the door to be sure she locked it after I went out to play, I was also protecting her, feeling responsible for her, and I was only six years old thinking that way.

The last place I remember vividly is the home in Hialeah. I remember a time when that same cousin was over and he was riding a big wheel along the complex's pool. He got a little too close and fell in. Ha ha. That was too funny, but he knew how to swim because our family enjoyed being around water—we're Bahamians on my dad's side. Our elders had a custom of throwing us in water when we were real young, so swimming came natural to us. We knew how to swim better than a lot of adults, and like I said before, my dad taught me to swim—he dunked me in our own family pool when I was a baby. But back to my cous'. He went all in—shoes, clothes, big wheel and all—and that was hilarious because it was summer and everybody in the whole complex was at the pool. I looked up, and my cousin was in the pool with the big wheel. We still laugh about that. It was from Hialeah that we left South Florida and moved to Tallahassee.

Once we adjusted to Tallahassee, we started feeling comfortable. We lived in a very nice, spacious condominium. It was in a really good neighborhood, my school was in walking distance, and—not to forget—I had some good friends who I walked to school with every day. As much as I'd liked Miami, I was really having fun in Tallahassee. Mom seemed happy too, so I thought it was where we would finally settle, a place where things were starting to level out. But it was not to be—even though we both had made a sacrifice, we let it all go. My mom and dad wanted our family back, and since my dad's business was based in Miami, it was best for us there. So we set our destination for back home to South Florida. We said goodbye to our friends and goodbye to Tallahassee.

We moved back to South Florida but not to Miami. We moved to Fort Lauderdale, in Broward County. My mom didn't want to move back to Miami, as she felt there were too many bad memories, too many bad influences, but as a kid, I didn't see it that way. To me, Miami was the best. It was nearly all I'd known up to that point, and Fort Lauderdale was completely foreign to me. I was a kid. All I cared about was that I was leaving my buddies like Juice, one of my closest friends in Tallahassee, and all the rest of them, but I was gonna be back with my dad. That's where my head was. Little did I know that this was a sign of how things would be and a big turning point in my life. My journey had begun.

Parents always want to do what's best for their children. As a parent, I know I do, and I know my parents did as well. So when your parents make decisions, as a child, you have to make the best of the resulting situations.

If you ever find yourself in a situation where you have to move back in with a parent, or you must learn to live with a new parent, who is not your biological parent, the one thing you have to always remind yourself—and the most important thing—is that it's all being done from a place of love. There ain't no books on this kind of stuff, and my mom wanted to do the right thing. In her mind, she was making the right decision because she had a child to raise, so she made the sacrifice to move back with my dad. Again, I was having to adjust, except this time, I was a little older and noticed things more. As a result, I went through a lot, and my mom was always supportive.

TO MAMA

'm so thankful to you, Mama. You never gave up on me. You fought through so much and prayed so many prayers. I don't have enough slots to text or even words to say. Not even the right hug or enough "I love you's" can explain. I thank you so much because I kind of understand now that I'm older; I know that the love and prayers of a mother for her child can break all yokes when she knows what she has instilled in him. The best way I can say it is: "Mama, in my eyes, all the achievements you have in life don't do justice or compare to what you have done and are still doing for and in my life; the life you saved—my life and all the things I will do."

BACK AT HOME

After moving back home and making the adjustments, my mom and I faced disappointment on that very first night in our new place, our new family apartment. There was no big welcome waiting—it was just me and mom. Dad was out. We had accepted leaving our lives up the road to come back home, but I never realized how much I would grow to resent that move back until much later in my life, when I looked back on the direction my life had taken.

Pops was making headway in his business and making pretty good money because I guess business was booming. We left that apartment and bought a home. It was a nice house, with a pool attached, and to anyone looking in from the outside, we had made it again. But this time, we were away from all our Miami family, and I was going to attend a totally different school from the one I'd always thought I would attend. I was adjusting again, but I didn't care—we were together as a family.

I soon accepted that no matter the changes to which I had to adjust, the friends and family I had to leave, and all that I had to do without, the one thing I did have was football. I played football all the way into my senior year of high school, and I did pretty well, held my own, and won a few trophies and all-county awards. The ones my parents were most proud of were the Scholastic Athlete Award and the Defensive Player of the Year Award for my team.

I loved football. It was my first love, and it kept me out of a lot of trouble because it gave me something to strive toward. I wasn't big or fast—all I had was love for the game and plenty heart. I loved playing with my teammates; we were individuals putting our talents together to achieve a common goal. There was no feeling like being on that field. The lights would come on, and we'd be on that field, strapped up and ready to lay the wood to anybody who had the ball. I didn't care how big they were—I was never intimidated by size, because I believe strongly it's the heart inside a man that measures him. Rest in peace to friends and teammates we lost through the years.

I really didn't have much interest in school. All it meant to me was playing ball, hanging with my friends, and getting the girls. I wasn't a dummy by any means—I just didn't see the point of school. I retained information, but I was just a bad test taker. I would study for the test and be ready on the day of, walk in class with confidence, and walk out with a score like 66 percent because it all looked foreign to me, the way they would ask the questions. It was like the test was designed to make you fail, like they were trick questions.

I think public school is so basic—at least when I was there, it didn't really seem to prepare you for anything, definitely not for life. It's not the teachers, in my opinion; it's the way the system is set up. I just didn't see how the stuff they were teaching me would help me earn a living, and although my situation was different—I had a college savings—what if I was someone who couldn't afford college? What good was some of that stuff? So the only time I went to class was when it was time for a report card, because I needed passing grades to play football. Plus, I had bought into the dream the world had sold me, of making it into the league. I dreamed of buying my mom the big house, with the Jaguar she's always wanted in the driveway.

Like I said, my pops found a nice home in a nice neighborhood. We never lived in slums or one of those types of neighborhoods that were designed to keep the people right where they were, but mostly everything and everybody I knew did live in one of those types of neighborhoods. So I felt the struggles of living in one because I was still surrounded by the mentality of that environment—I was a part of it by association. So like everybody else, I believed that football was gonna be my ticket away from everything that wasn't right.

My mom is an educator, and she stressed the importance of education. My dad is a businessman and stressed the need of me becoming independent and having my own. There's a song by the great Aretha Franklin, "God Bless the Child Who Got His Own". That's what my parents instilled in me. Together they taught me a lot of things about life. My mom taught me the importance of knowing who you are and where you come from, as well as pride in being a black man—and in not joining those who degrade other black men or blacks in general. She would say, "Never air your dirty linen"—in other words, always be supportive and loyal to your family and never go against them in public. My dad would say, "Look a man in the eye when you talk to him. Have a firm handshake." My mom would say, "Keep your shoulders back and head high." She called that "keeping a high-air" attitude. She'd say, "Always look up, not down, and never let anyone make you feel inferior. Always speak up for yourself— stand up for what you believe. Never back down from anyone, and if you have to resort to fighting, make sure that person knows they have been in a fight and who they were fighting: bring it to them so hard that they'll think twice about trying to fight you again. Be a leader, not a follower. Always love yourself, because there's nobody else like you in the world. Never be afraid to be yourself, and always, always treat others as you want to be treated." These are all things my parents spoke into me as a child and a young man growing into manhood. My mom would say a lot of these things close to my ear when I was small after saying prayers for bed—words I went to sleep on. These are lessons I didn't understand then, but they stayed with me. I speak some of those same lessons to my children today.

Even so, during these times when it was just me and Mom, with all these lessons I received from her, as I became more of man, I realized that there were lessons and answers only the man of the house could give me. That was one of the main reasons why my mom felt it was important for us to be back as a family.

The family institution is powerful. It's like a ladder. The family affects the neighborhood, which affects the community, which affects the city, which affects the county, the state, and ultimately the entire nation. The man is the head of the family, and as the saying goes, "You kill the head, and everything under it falls too." I believe this is why the enemy's first attack is to try to destroy the man, the head. So while the man of the house was working hard, as the young man of the house, I was learning about life on my own. It was confusing because to family and friends we were an example of a successful family, reaching higher heights, and that was mostly because of my dad. His success was the template of how you can start from nothing and make it good, and for that, I'm proud.

My dad changed his life for the better. He had to learn a lot of how to survive from growing up in the streets of Sugar Hill, an old hood in Miami, Florida. I know he's a real man, a strong man—just some wrong turns happened. A lot of what he learned he did on his own because he never even knew his dad. He was raised by my granddaddy, his stepdad, and that man was a true character. He was something else. My granddad was tough as nails, and he was who my dad knew as his dad. In fact, he was the only man some of my cousins knew as a father figure. He was a good man. He died of cancer when I was about ten years old. But even with Granddad there, still my dad learned to fend for himself growing up. He learned the streets, and when he was a teenager, the streets got him in trouble. Once he got through that, long before I was born, he made up his mind that that life was behind him, and he studied and became the first black man to become a mortgage broker in Miami, and that was a big deal.

My mom taught me how to cook and clean during those times when Dad wasn't around, but when he was, he owned the grill. He is a master on that thing. Those were some of the best family times, and he made the best conch salad you ever tasted—that's a Bahamian favorite. I didn't pick up too many tips back then, as those were my middle and high school years, and school and sports were keeping me busy. Sometimes it felt like I was in a single-parent home. I'm not talking monetarily—my dad made good money, but that came with a sacrifice. He was building a business and handling these personal challenges. I'm sure it was stressful, so in no way did anything come easy for him.

My mom and I spent a lot of time together. She never discussed the emptiness. All she did was step up. She taught me how to wash and fold my clothes, how to clean, how to sort through situations I might face, and generally how to take care of myself. We talked about all kinds of things—even girls, how to detect the good ones from the not-so-good ones. I did a lot with my dad as well. He and I went to football games together and had talks, but it was during the after-school hours when my mom and I spent so much time together, the evening hours during homework and after-school activities. In fact, she was the one who took me to my first football tryout. I remember it like it was today. (I'll get to that story later.)

Well, it was time to start driving, and I learned to drive on a stick shift. My mom and I used to go to this empty parking lot close to our neighborhood, and she would let me practice. During these times, I was learning some very necessary life skills, like how to be independent, especially in my relationships with women. Mom and I talked about a lot of things during this time, such as learning how to do things for yourself as a means to avoid unhealthy relationships, in addition to learning how to treat others well. Being unhappy in a relationship and staying in it because you are helpless, can't fend for yourself, and wouldn't be able to cook if your partner left you are all wrong reasons for staying. On the other hand, my mom wanted me to learn those same skills so I would be a partner in a relationship and treat a woman special—to not worry about my ego when I would do things like prepare a meal, do laundry, and do anything else for the good of the relationship.

So I learned a lot about growing into manhood from my mom, and I'm sure that could be the story of a lot of black men, my dad included. Of course, it's always better when fathers are around more, but that wasn't the case in my home, so I had to man up and follow my own lead as I got older. It's concerning, even ironic, how people misuse the phrase or advice *man up* when a man talks of challenges he's dealt with throughout his life. Whether his situation is the result of choices he's made or ones that were made for him, that's always people's go-to and quickest answer, it seems, before they really hear what he is saying. He's not complaining, whining, or making excuses, just in need of a listening ear and some relatable understanding, but the first and sometimes only answer is "You need to man up." If people only knew just how much I had to man up for real and always, always with God's grace—I rose to the challenge.

I remember my first encounter with the law. My mom slapped me across the head right in front of the police when she came to pick me up. She was so mad and wasn't about to lose me to the streets. When she picked me up, she was furious. "Boy, what the hell are you doing stealing when we make sure you have money in your pocket every day?" I was embarrassed in front of my friends and all, but that was just the tough love I needed at that time.

I now see on this journey of mine that so many of the things visible about me are a result of seeds that were planted deep in my soul, things that kept me going and are why I'm still here. I can embrace some of the dark days, the struggles, setbacks, and detours, because I now know it's all just so temporary. If we listen close enough through all the noise, chaos, hustlin', and bustlin', the voice of God is there in that still and quiet place in the midst of the storm. The quietness is His voice.

FIRST LEG OF THE RACE

Having good memories is a way to create happiness, because when you hold on to those good memories, they help you through those rough times. In this world, we live moment to moment, and this moment is all we have—it will never, ever be repeated. This time, Wednesday, February 12, 2014, at 2:45 p.m., will never be lived again. What we have at a particular time is just what we have—where we are is just where we are—and when that moment is gone, it becomes history and a part of our journey. Then we move on to the next slot.

A good way to look at this is as a new beginning rather than as a loss. At any moment, we choose and let the past be just what it is—the past. This lets us know that everything in the flesh is temporary; only the spirit is forever living. God is a new beginning, and at all times, He's forever moving forward, forever creating, so at any time, if we choose to reach for Him, we can change our direction and fate, change our state of mind, and eventually change our lives.

As my journey continues, so do my struggles, but the one thing that remains constant is that I know I came from strength, and the wisdom that's gained is priceless. My hope is that the lessons I have learned and am still learning will one day be used to help somebody—that if people relate to anything I've said here, they'll have gained something that may help them get through some of their challenges.

When my life is over, my dash will be finished, and I hope I will have made an impact in this world—huge ripples, just like I always wanted—but for now, I have to stop and think about things. I'm still young in my life, and my story isn't even close to being complete. And I realize that life is full of second chances.

I was afraid of life's setbacks and failures, and as I am living through my struggles, I'm learning how not to be in a hurry, how not to always feel like I have to move fast to make up for the time lost, how not to always feel like everything has to happen my way, right then and in my time. I've gotta know how to be blessed man because I'm realizing that some of the toughest times ain't even came yet. But they're on the track, and I'm just on the first leg of this race called life.

HUNGRY FOR MORE CHRIST

Music was one of the things that kept me calm. I love music, and you can find out a lot about a man by his music. I feel strongly that God spoke to me in my teenage years through music, and that was one of the connections I had with my dad. When I was young, I could tell he knew everything about music. I can remember this huge collection he had. It was kept in a very large custom-built entertainment center that sat in a step-down area in the family room of our first house, the one where I was born.

Music was always playing in our home, so my dad's music became mine because I wanted any attachment to him. That's how sons are when it comes to dads. They play a big part, and the developmental years when a boy is becoming a man are the most pivotal. As a young kid, I treasured every minute with him—his music, his sports, and his likes were mine too. But as the years brought more struggles (or maybe not more—maybe they were the same struggles and I was just getting older and becoming more aware, especially after coming back from Tallahassee), and as certain issues grew, changes were made. We moved from that house, from that area, and from the memories and moved to Broward County, a totally different area, away from my cousins and everything that was familiar to me. Even though it was only a short drive away, it still wasn't Miami. Not having an older brother to see how he would've done it was a challenge; I had to make my own way, determine my own identity, and set my own path, and I started young. My journey was taking a new path now.

When I was thirteen, my dad and I had the talk about sex, and he wanted to know if I was active yet. I wasn't, but my dad was starting the conversation, opening the book of life that every young man needs and should have from his dad—the talk about sex. I think my dad was trying to give me the talk he had never been fortunate enough to have with his dad. All I knew about sex was as a li'l' git (a li'l' brother) hanging around with my cousins, so I had that street knowledge, but at that particular time in my life, looking back, I feel I would've benefited from my dad talking more about what was in the Bible than about sex.

I'm not saying he never discussed the Bible—he definitely did that. And he would always answer my questions, anything about animals and nature, and sometimes we would just take a trip for no reason—no holiday, no birthday, just take a trip to the Everglades or Lion Country Safari when I was a li'l' git. He would use those long rides to just teach me—no answering a beeper, just answering any questions I had about how things started with Christ. At that particular time in my life, when I was trying to learn who I was, I didn't realize that knowing about Christ was where my hunger was. Now that I'm older and I have children, especially sons, I know Bible lessons are better for teaching them about the direction they will go. That talk with my dad had its place; I just feel that with all the teachings he had already been giving me about the Bible and about God, praying with me during that time would have been better. I felt

I needed to be taught God's way instead of getting that traditional talk. But like I said, he did it the only way he knew and still gave me more than his dad had ever given him, and I love him for that.

It's necessary to show the importance of the Word on all levels of life, even when it's sex. Sure, I could've read what the Bible had to say about it for myself, but since I always got so much from my dad any time he talked about the Bible, as I reflect on the world and my sons today, I know it would have had a different impact coming from him than if I'd just read it for myself.

When it came to sex, just like a lot of other things, I had gotten off the perch early. My feelings had not caught up with my actions when I became sexually active, which was very early in my life, when I was fifteen—although, unfortunately, in today's times, that's not early anymore. I was only experimenting, without intimacy, and intimacy is a very important part of a relationship between a man and a woman. Their closeness depends on familiarity and friendship. It connects them. Intimacy is what makes a relationship. I guess that all comes with maturity.

We have religion, which is just on the surface, traditions that are not personal, and we have an intimate relationship with God, which is to know, trust, and love Him and to interact, share, converse, and connect with Him on a personal level. This is the kind of relationship God deserves with His children. We should have that same relationship with our children and bond with them through communication, honesty, and friendship, which is a form of intimacy. They should feel they can be safe and free to talk with us about anything, knowing nothing will ever make us stop loving them and that we're always there. This, to me, is very important in raising children, and even if they live away from you, they should still know it. As parents, we should be the first people they come to for anything.

God created sex, and it's a beautiful thing. So is bringing a child into this world when done so in marriage. It is even a form of worship because that's one of the ways God created for us to express our love toward each other, and again, it is designed for the institution of marriage.

Nowadays, we live in such a sex-craved society—sex is everywhere and wide open. You can't even go to the store without seeing a poster of a half-naked woman or a man with no shirt, flexing his muscles, advertising something that has nothing to do with what they're selling. But sex sells in this world, and unfortunately, the youth are not protected. Kids see and hear things they're not equipped to process, and curiosity eventually gets the best of us all. It is in music and radio commercials, on billboards and television—everywhere— and with social media, sex through advertising is all too easy to access, not to mention pornography.

So there I was in my early years experiencing sex. I don't know if it was just in my blood or if I was just a flirt, but I feel it came honest. I love women—we all did. In my grandma's house in Liberty City, my granddad knocked down the partition wall between their bedroom and another room. I don't know what the reason was— maybe he intended to add something, but that was my grandpa. So the now connecting room was my two uncles' room. I remember my cousins and I used to sneak into their room and just look at the *Playboy* magazines. We were no more than five or six years old, and there we were, getting our early exposure to sex. I think every little boy at some point is curious and gets a hold of his big brother's or his uncle's or somebody's magazines. Please don't think that I'm glorifying things I did at this young age, and I am not trying to degrade women. My purpose here is only to emphasize how important it is in these days—with our kids having so much exposure, much more than I had—to talk to your kids about what the Bible has to say about sex, love, and marriage. They may not understand that part of the Bible, and may be too young to even have questions, but when they do, they'll know that you taught them God's plan for them and that the answers to their questions are not of this world but of His word, with your guidance. I believe that misdirection of any kind can lead to wrong choices of every kind.

Well, as you might have guessed by now, with roots like that, it wouldn't be long before I would get a young woman pregnant outside marriage. Thankfully, for the both of us, we were finished with high school, but still, a baby before marriage is not smart. The flip side of having sex before the intended time—having it too early—is that it becomes watered down, and when you finally get with a woman you have feelings for and want to have a meaningful, mature relationship with, you almost have to relearn everything you knew about it because intimacy was missing before. So my advice—and I feel I'm in a position to give some—is to just wait for sex and do what the Good Book says. You're really not missing out on anything.

MIXED PRIORITIES

I mentioned earlier that when I left for college, I didn't have a clue of what I wanted to be. All I knew was I wanted to keep playing football, smoking, drinking, and getting every woman I was attracted to. I knew it wasn't right, but I'm just being real. God was working on me then, and he still ain't finished with me to this day. I had a plan, but I wasn't true to it. I knew I wanted to play football, but I wasn't doing things that would make me successful in that game.

If you want something as much as I wanted football, you have to reevaluate your priorities. One of mine should have been to have an idea of what I wanted to study in college. That should have been my priority, but it wasn't. So I didn't go about college the right way. All I did know *fo' sho* was that I didn't want to repeat the mistakes of my dad, because I knew he didn't want that for me either. I had basically reached manhood with an internal battle between trying to live by the ways my parents taught me and doing the things I had learned of the world—what it really was and what it was steadily showing me each day.

I left for college in 1996 and dropped out in 1999, angry with the world. When I left for college, I had hopes and expectations, but

I came back home confused and in disarray, looking at my life as a big disappointment. I had flunked out of college and in turn failed to start the future my parents had envisioned for me. My mom had been putting money away since I was in elementary school; it was a college plan she and my dad had invested in early. I'm not blaming my failures on anyone but me. My son was dead, a lot of my friends had been shot and killed, and I didn't make the football team, and to top all that, things at home with my parents still weren't going too well. I began to realize at that time that life was full of adversities and how we handle them is what gives us character.

GOOD MEMORIES

One of the happiest memories I had with my cousins was going fishing with my grandma, but anything I did with my grandma was cool. I would love sick days because I knew that meant I would get to go to her house, and those were just the best days. She would make me Cream of Wheat for breakfast, and it would just be the two of us together. The funny thing was that when I would go back home with my mom, I would ask her to make Cream of Wheat for me, and for the longest, she tried—would use all the same ingredients—and still I never got that taste like at Grandma's. Now when I think back, the ingredient that was missing from Mama's was not a certain spice, and it wasn't the wrong brand—nothing like that. Only thing missing was my grandma's touch making it.

My grandma was a nurse, and she was old school, one of those real grandmas who was from the Bahamas—Cat Island, to be exact. She was a natural-born nurturer, a true grandma type, who did things the natural way. My grandma was so real and so authentic, a one-of-a-kind good lady. Even though she worked, she never drove a day in her life, so she had to get a ride wherever she went, and believe me—she never had a problem getting anyplace. Everyone loved that lady.

When I was real young, I couldn't properly say the word *Grandma*, so I called her Bim-Ma. Ha ha, it sounded like Grandma to me, so that became my name for her.

Grandma died in August 2011, the same year my third son was born. In fact, I met my wife the same week of my grandma's funeral. I know that may sound complicated, but you'll see what I mean later.

When I was a kid, my cousins and I did everything together and went everywhere together. We were like brothers. My aunts even gave us all baths together. We fought one another and fought other kids together. That's the bond I have with my cousins; we don't act brand new with one another, because we know one another so well. We go so far back, and we love one another. One of the many things we did for fun was sneak into a local high school just to have the security guard chase us out. There was a li'l' clique of guys we hung with.

One day, the way I remember it, we were caught by security, and as usual, they threw us out, but the problem this time was that one of our friends had snitched on us when security caught him. He told them where we were because we would usually be in the library, gym, or cafeteria. When we got outside, we saw him up ahead walking, and one of the kids with us picked up a bottle and slung it. He had pretty good aim, too, because if that kid hadn't turned around in time to duck, it would've hit him right in the back of the head. Eventually, we caught up to where he was, and the two started fighting. But one thing about the hood: when you fight one kid, there is always somebody else you're going to have to tango with. This dude left and got his older brother, who then put a good beatdown on the one who had beat his li'l' brother, but he wasn't with us. Then word got back to that kid's older brother, and he jumped out the crowd and started whalin' on the other kid's older brother.

Later that day, I heard that he got shot by someone else who had ties with the kid's older brother, who he had put the beatdown on. If you're reading this and you know the hood, you're not confused; you already know that's how it goes. That's when I learned that no matter how big, bad, and tough we are or think we are, there's always one out there who's tougher, always a bigger fish. We all got to "wear a' ass whuppin'" at least once in our lives.

REACHING DEEP INSIDE

N o matter what we did differently from day to day, the one thing we always found time to do every day was play football. We would play tackle football on grass with rocks, pipes, broken glass, and all in it. You may have gotten a few bumps, bruises, cuts, and scrapes, but you were having fun, and you were learning that scars are just a part of growing up.

Family, if I could do anything over in my life, it would be to go back to those days I played football—Little League and high school. I would've played every play like it was my last if I'd known then that it wouldn't last forever. There are plays I go through in my mind that I could've done better. But I didn't have much of what scouts look for in football players—size and speed. I just did the best I could and played as hard as I could. I left it all on the field.

If I could've done things differently, I wouldn't have been so hard on myself whenever I messed up or didn't make the big play, because that kept me from enjoying the whole experience more. So don't ever be too hard on yourself—save that for others. But I need to be satisfied that I played with heart and that I always did my job. I wasn't a superstar player, just a good, consistently solid player.

When we lived in Tallahassee, I didn't play Optimist football, as my mom wasn't able to find a league, but there was baseball. I never liked baseball, but I had to play some type of sports, had to compete, because it was in my blood, so I played baseball. But, thankfully, when we got back to South Florida, football was everywhere.

The first organized team I played on was at Lauderhill's Paul Turner Park. My coach was a police officer. In fact, he was the first black cop I ever saw, and he used to stutter. It was funny because he would call us *knucklehead* when we weren't paying attention: "Knu-knu-knu-knucklehead," he would say. And even though it sounded funny coming out, we never made fun of him; we knew he meant business. But he was coaching for all the right reasons—to help kids. He was a good coach.

There was a kid out there we called Mighty Mouse because he was small, but he could do a backflip with no running start, just stand still, jump, and flip. So many kids I played with had major talent. South Florida always has been a part of the state known for football, and down here, football was religion. It was a way out, and it was where some kids had their only attachment to a male figure. Football was everything, and all the inner cities were full of talent. A lot of the kids I played with all the way up to high school had enough talent to tear the NFL up, but because of their environment, some of their backgrounds, and the attitudes that went with them, many of them never made it close.

There were three kids who were the fastest at the whole park, and every night after practice, we would race against one another. At first, they would leave me in their dust, but as I kept racing against the competition, it made me better. Eventually, I beat the third-fastest and then the second-fastest kids, but there was one I could never beat. I couldn't beat Mighty Mouse—no one could. This kid was really fast. Every night after practice, we would all hang around and challenge him. I would come close—real close, at times—but he would always pull away from me in the end. There was a lesson in that, and I carry it with me every day: Everywhere we go, there's always going to be someone faster, bigger, stronger, and smarter. In everything there is always someone just a little better. But when we surround ourselves with people who make us rise up instead of lower down, it brings out the best in us. We'll never be the best at everything we do, but if we give our absolute best at everything we do, then the results don't matter.

Some people are used to being the best because they put themselves in a talent pool that is nowhere near their level. Then the first time they go to next level, where the talent pool is equal or greater, they get a rude awakening. It destroys their confidence, and they immediately become discouraged because they had relied only on their talent to get them by. They had never been put in a position where they had to rely on what was inside them, which is heart, plenty of heart to give it your all.

Sometimes that's all you've got to pull you through—the heart that you can make it, no matter what. Racing against the fastest kid every day taught me how to dig deep inside myself and pull it out at an early age. When I think about it, my parents could've had me playing at some other park with kids who didn't look like me, where I would've been the token. I might have been the best at everything and the superstar, but what would that have taught me about reaching deep down inside myself? This applies not just to sports but to everything in life.

I believe that being raised up in inner cities may have had its downsides in many cases, but no matter—it still produced some of the toughest and most fierce competitors. We faced adversities our whole lives in everything we did as kids, so sometimes being constantly immersed in situations where we had to scrap and use all we had inside us was how we survived. It's still the same in a lot of areas.

It's amazing, the things you learn as a boy that stay with you, because I learned a lot of what I did on defense from playing as a kid what we called *murder ball*. Just playing around the neighborhoods, no organized teams or nothin', every man for himself, and with one simple rule—just one: whoever catches the ball's gotta run, and everybody in the game's gonna come to "take his head off"— meaning hit him so hard that he never wants the ball again. Ha ha. Big fun!

I finally started playing Optimist football at Lauderhill Park for three years, and then I went to Lauderdale Lakes Park, which was known for winning championships and still is to this day. I mean, when it came to Lakes, the needle registered *full* on talent. Lakes is a feeding ground for some of the major and most popular high schools in the area. Playing at this park just made me better, and I found a way to get on that field every game. Not only did I love playing football; I was a student of the game. I studied its history and had a true interest in it—I was like a walking football encyclopedia. I could tell you almost anything and everything about football. I played every position on the field at one point or another, except quarterback. I could not throw for nothin' (ha ha). I played on both sides of the ball, but my true game was defense because I liked to be the one to deliver the blow more than I did the one taking it.

ONE-ON-ONE WITH BARRY SANDERS

I remember when I was about eight years old, we were at a cookout at the home of my parents' friend, whose husband used to coach pro football. When I told the man I liked to play defense, he said, "That's smart. Be the one to give the blows instead of taking them." But the exciting part of that day was that both Barry Sanders and Evander Holyfield were at that same cookout. I had a great time, and I have pictures with them. It was the best experience. I'll never forget having a close-up, one-on-one talk with the great Barry Sanders—and just so you know, he agreed with the advice the coach gave me. Loving football the way I did, that afternoon I spent with Barry Sanders felt like time stood still. Like I said, my young years were good, and my dad was around a lot. He even took me to meet Sugar Ray Leonard, who I also took a picture with and got a chance to see sparring, but football was my passion.

It was my contact sport of choice, and I loved to deliver the hit. I loved playing defense. I always felt that playing offense was for the pretty boys, ha ha. They scored all the points and got the cheers from the crowd, but defense was gritty, dirty, and tough, and that's exactly what I wanted. It's what I was, and it was why I loved football. But no matter what side of the ball you played, offense or defense, you had to have two things: love for contact and plenty heart. You had to know how to get back up after getting smacked silly and had to learn to deal with pain and be conditioned, because like one of my high school teachers told me, "Fatigue makes cowards of us all." You had to be disciplined and a team player, and have tough skin, because coaches were gonna yell, curse, jump in your face, criticize—whatever it took to motivate you to play the game and win. But now I know, after being on that side, coaching young men as well, it was all love—tough love.

Barry Sanders , Evander Holyfield, Cornelius Bennett, and Alonzo Highsmith invited me in photo at our friend's house

Sugar Ray Leonard in town training for a fight

The game of football wasn't for everybody, though, and if you ever played the game or know someone who did, you know the separation time came every year when the pads went on. The first two weeks are just conditioning, running and getting in shape, but then comes the day the hitting starts. That's when the teams always trimmed down, because a lot of kids who'd looked like stars during training time, who looked good and conditioned, never came back after the pads started clackin'. Hitting was what I had a reputation for because I ain't care how big you was, you come in my area, I'm gonna lay the wood to you, make you know I was there, make you timid about coming to my side again. Rules of the game have always been that the team who hits the hardest is the team who wins— intimidation. Make the other team's players so intimidated that they don't want the ball in their hands. Whoever got that ball knew they was gonna get hit and get hit hard.

CHANGING THE GAME

A s with life, as with everything, football changed. It moved far away from the way we played. Rules now are to protect the players, and that's a good thing. There were very few rules to protect players back then; when you played football, you were making a choice. You knew when you stepped out on the field that getting hurt was one of the consequences. But it's necessary nowadays because guys are so much bigger, faster, and stronger, and with all the weight-gain supplements and advanced, elite workout programs, it's like trains colliding—somebody is bound to get hurt—so they had to do something to protect those guys out there.

When I played, it was a little more natural. I didn't think much about gettin' hurt, because if you play continuously, you're gonna get hurt. You had to go 100 percent every play because it's a game of motion, but I still loved it. I played organized football a total of twelve years and only lay on the field hurt one time, and that was because I was just curious. I wanted to know what the procedure was when you got hurt and trainers and coaches came out on the field to you: What did they say? What questions did they ask? What did they actually do for you? These are things I always wanted to know (ha ha). I was weird and curious that way. There was this time when

I was really hurt. I'd had the worst injuries and played through them because I never wanted to be out of the game. I loved it that much. But this particular time, I knew we had the game won, so I decided to take care of myself—didn't feel I was letting my team down— and stayed down to be attended to for a change and to satisfy my curiosity at the same time. Today, when players get concussions, it's taken very seriously, and every precaution is taken to avoid them, but there wasn't as much information on head injuries back then.

So there may have been times when what we thought were just hard hits to the head—the ones where everyone in the whole stadium would stand up and cheer after you laid one out ("Ooh, did you hear that hit?")—were actually concussions. We just got up, maybe slowly, but we had to get up, shake the cobwebs off on each play until our heads got a little clearer, and maybe sit out a play.

When I look back, I'm sure I had a few concussions in high school, but I didn't know what a concussion was—at least I didn't know that's what it's called. It was a mixed-up kind of feeling, a feeling like being in another world, disoriented, like in the twilight zone or another dimension. In other words, I was still on the field, but I wasn't. My eyesight was like looking at television through dim lighting, faded out and a li'l' blurry, not precise or clear at all. My memory was faint, and I really didn't know what I was doing.

As I'm sitting here recalling every detail of what that felt like, I'm thinking how good it is that they are now taking better care of these young boys and girls playing ball and are more precautious. I'm thankful that they know the seriousness of head injuries and the lingering side effects. I know I have experienced a few of such side effects from time to time. Out of nowhere, I would black out. I'd be awake, my eyes wide open, but everything would be dim and black, to the point where I couldn't see anything. Like someone was dimming the tint on a television screen until it was all the way black. It's hard to explain. It was weird, but if you've ever had a concussion, you know just what I'm talking about.

The point of all this is to help young men who play this game. Don't get so caught up that you allow it to take over your common sense. If you get hurt, if you get rattled by someone delivering a hard hit, don't feel that it makes you soft to speak up about it, especially if there are any lingering effects from that hit. Tell someone. Other people have no other way of knowing what's going on inside your head. It can be dangerous.

I remember crossing the street once, I couldn't see anything—it was kind of scary. I heard horns honking, but I couldn't see anything, no matter how wide I tried to open my eyes. This was an experience you don't want. Personally, I thought at times it was also the result of drugs and alcohol. I'm just being real. So my advice as a player and as someone who has overindulged in the wrong things one too many times is to take care of yourself and your body. Don't be so hungry for time in the game that you forsake your body. Live to play another game, as there will be more. Speak up when you're hurt.

I didn't play football during my eighth-grade year in middle school. My bones had developed some kind of disease in my kneecap—at least that's how the doctor described it. All I can remember is that my knees hurt bad and were very tender to the slightest touch. The doctor gave me a shot from a very long needle, right into the bone, where the pain was most severe. It seemed like he held that needle in my bone for a good five minutes so he could inject the medicine. Afterward, he put a cast on one leg that went from my hip to my foot, along with a removable brace on the other leg, the same length as the cast. Of course he gave me a set of crutches to complete my package. I think orthopedic doctors are gonna give you a cast whether you need one or not, ha ha. That's what they do.

I was in that contraption for six weeks. I missed sports so much that those six weeks felt like six years. I couldn't stand being immobile. But I was never one to stay down long. I remember that after a while, I was on the basketball court shooting the ball with my whole leg cast. Even though the doctor had said no activities, my stubbornness would never let me accept from anyone that I could not do something—no such thing as *I can't*. I wasn't able to run up and down the court, but I hobbled on one leg. I never knew I could until I saw some friends playing ball on the court and I hobbled up, told them to pass me the ball, and was out there playing basketball with a cast on my leg. That stubborn part of my character—that part I later recognized as my will to keep going, to never stay down, to never let nothin' hold me back or let anyone tell me what I can or cannot do—pushed me through a lot of obstacles in my life. You have that same will in you.

I played basketball for my school's team. I liked it, and I was a starter when I played, but my sport was football. I could not wait to get back on that field. The cast came off, and I was cleared to play again. I remember how my leg was so weak and how it used to have this stinky odor from having been wrapped in that cast with so little air for so long. But as stinky as it was, nothing was worse than the itching. My leg would itch so bad at times I would have to scratch it with a hanger.

STRAPPING ON THE PADS

I was starting high school the next year, and I could stay on Optimist level or go up and play high school ball. I decided to play high school football, and I was headed to Plantation High School. This was a school I had never heard of in my life, much less considered playing for. At our school, we were the Colonels—you know, Plantation ... Colonels ... get it? The *plantation* alone made me think of slavery, and then for us to be named the Colonels just didn't do it for me. I hated that name—absolutely *hated* it. I mean, I was raised on the history of our people—my parents, grandparents, aunts, and whole family always talked about the struggles and pride of black people—so you can imagine how it felt for me to play for a team called the Colonels and for a school with the name Plantation. Besides, the only schools I had heard of in Broward County were Dillard High, Blanche Ely High, and Boyd Anderson High. I was raised up in Miami, a product of Dade County, and all I knew were the Miami Northwestern Senior High Bulls. When I lived in Carol City, it was the Rockets of Carol City High. In Little Haiti, it was the Red Raiders of Edison High. But my whole family had all gone to either Miami Northwestern High School or Central High. So I knew I was going to be either a Bull or a Rocket. I ain't know nothin' 'bout no Colonels, but I guess in their attempt to move me to a better environment, my parents moved to Broward, and Plantation High was where I went to school. My parents never knew how I felt because I respected them, so I respected their decisions.

All high schools usually have varsity and junior varsity teams, but I didn't know nothin' about that. So there I was on Plantation High School's football field. This brings me back to the day I was telling you about with my tryouts. My mom and I went out to practice one day to find out how to sign up. We went to the first group we saw, which was varsity—juniors and seniors—but it was my first year. My mom said to me, "I don't know, Brent. These boys look pretty big." Of course I said, "I ain't worried 'bout that. I can play wit 'em." Remember I was used to playing street ball, or "murder football," ha ha. By that time, one of the coaches saw us and came over to talk. We told him what we were trying to do. He looked at me, looked at my mom, smiled, and said, "Maybe football's not the route you want to go." That reminds me of a real close friend of my mom's—for our purposes and to avoid using her real name, I'm going to refer to her as Meggie—who I called Aunt Meg. She used to crack, or tease, on me and say, "You too small to play football. You need to be playing tennis or golf or something!" She used to tutor me in my worst subject, math. I was failing it before I got help from her, but she really knew that math. I think performing poorly in math gave me another reason to not want to be in school. My aunt Meg was cool, though. She was real patient with me and made it fun while I was learning because she was funny without knowing it and without trying. She used to crack on everybody, especially my mom and her best friend, who used to always be over there. But Aunt Meg got hit with breast cancer and died some years later. I miss her.

She had a huge heart and was so genuine. If she liked you, she liked you, because there was nothing fake about her.

"Maybe football's not the route you want to go"—I couldn't believe what I had heard! To someone who loved football as much as I did, those words were like a stab in my heart. There I was, standing there listening to this dude, and I remember thinking that I might not get to play based on what that coach was saying. He was courteous—wasn't disrespectful at all, just giving me his advice. It was not something I wanted to hear, though. But that didn't matter. I ain't never been no big dude. I just knew football was my game and I was going to play.

As we were leaving, the strangest thing happened. A different coach came running us down, and I don't know what he saw, but he told me to sign up for junior varsity. Now those were the words I was more prepared to hear. I made up in my mind right then and there that he would never regret having given me a chance.

I would be learning a whole new position, that of safety. I was a freshman—new to the school, didn't know anybody—but I beat out the starter from the previous year in tryouts and played in the first game. That was my first time playing since sitting out the previous year, and I played that game like a madman. I must've had at least fifteen tackles, as well as caused some fumbles. Man! I was all over the field. We ended up winning that game. I was a starter at safety position for the rest of the year. We ended the season with a 6–2 record.

I never realized how so much of who I became was from those years. I learned a lot about myself. Talk about making lemonade out of lemons. I had to suck it up and come to grips with the fact that even though I was in unfamiliar surroundings, going to a school where I didn't know anybody, and playing for a school whose name I hated, I had a choice to either allow my anger to cloud what was ahead of me or go out there, put all that secondary stuff behind, and play like a Miami Northwestern High Bull in a Plantation's Colonel uniform. And that's exactly what I did! I decided to make the name Brent Ellis, strong safety, number 16, be a part of every opposing team's coach locker-room talk. I realized that having passion for something and believing in yourself help you overcome obstacles that you once thought unmovable.

The next year, varsity's head coach moved me and some other teammates up to varsity. I didn't start, because the man ahead of me was pretty good and he was a senior. Those in the senior group ahead of us were "thugged out ", that means street tough, in their own way. I mean, they were a solid group of ballplayers, cool and down to earth. They were always pulling pranks like players usually do in locker rooms, and they loved our class because, like them, our class had moved up too—"thugged out" and solid in our own way. They actually welcomed our group so much because Plantation was historically a white school, with a white football team, and in my opinion, they always were sorry and were always getting their butts kicked by all the black schools. That changed once they started to integrate and recruit from neighborhoods with kids who looked like me. By the time we got out there, it was a mixed school, but the football team was mostly black kids from inner-city neighborhoods.

That year, we beat Dillard High, one of the best high schools in the county in sports. Yep, that's right. The Colonels beat the Panthers. We finished with a 7–3 record and made it to the playoffs. We got beat the first round by Boyd Anderson High. Now it was my junior year, 1995, and it was my time to start. For the privacy of not using names here, I'll refer to this senior as "Jake". He was like a mentor on that field to me. He said, "Look here, man," "we play stud safety, we free to roam—all we do is hit and lay people out." That was cool with me because that's all I wanted to do anyway. Man! We had a hell of a team, and we were all cool with one another, like brothers. My dawg" Sweats" played receiver. That dude caught everything that came his way." J. C., Crow", and "Red" played receiver, running back, and full back, and "Slice" was quarterback. Defense was made up of a bunch of crazy people. "Juice", "Scat", and "D. J". played linebacker." Stack" was probably the most underrated linebacker around, one of the best in the county, and that boy was a headhunter." Slades" and "TNT" played with me in secondary." Slades" had transferred from another school and was the youngest of three brothers, the eldest of whom were playing in the NFL and at the top of their game. In other words, they were tearing it up. But one thing about Slades that I respected was that he didn't ride on the coattails of his brothers by expecting special treatment. He was just the opposite; he was one of the boys who paid his dues like everybody else, and he let what he did on the field speak for him. "Slick" and" Frogman" were freshmen but got a lot of playing time because they took the game seriously and played ball. (All the names used here were made-up names in place of the actual names of players on the team.)

I played strong safety, but I was up next to the linebacker, so I got a lot of tackles and a lot of big hits. I was one of the small guys on the team, but my intangibles were love and passion for the game, knowledge of the game, and plenty, plenty of heart. Everybody on the team came from Lakes Park, Western Tigers, or Southwest Saints, all the best Optimist parks in Lauderdale.

We finished the season 8–2 and got beat during the second round of playoffs by some team from up the road in Melbourne, Florida. In my senior year, we were unstoppable, man! We were blowing teams out 61–0. Coaches were taking us out by the second half, and our second string would finish the game. It was an exciting year! We finished the season 10–0. Undefeated! We were the first team in more than thirty years to go undefeated for that school.

Then the playoffs came, and I had to go into my murder-ball mentality because we were playing Miami Northwestern in the third round. This was the school of the community where I was raised, the school I was supposed to attend, so I had mixed feelings. On the one hand, I was playing for a school where I had no ties—one that was named after slave owners, in my opinion—one where the only attachments I had were the guys I played ball with every week, and I was about to play against kids I grew up playing murder ball with in the streets of Liberty City in Miami. If that wasn't bad enough, my family from Dade County came up for the game, so even though I wasn't playing as a Bull, we had the better record. The game was really hyped. All the sports people did stories about it for weeks prior. The crowd was huge. About ten to fifteen thousand attended, so we had to play at Lockhart Stadium, a large county stadium. I had never played in front of a crowd that big in my life! It was a good, close game, but we lost 10–6.

That was the end of my high school football career. Little did I know it would be the last game I ever played.

I never was on a team that won a championship, but I never played on a losing team either. I also got to play with a lot of good dudes who should have made it to the NFL, but there's a lot more stuff going on behind the game that controls that. One thing I did take with me from playing with my team, took with me through life, is that all I gotta do is play my position the best I can, and my plays will come to me. Let the man next to me play his position, and his plays will come to him. If we're on the same team, we all win, but I've gotta play my position, not that of the man next to me, because it's something I bring to help make the team complete. That can apply to every phase of life.

One thing's for sure. My dad made it a point to be at every game I played. He was proud of me, so he told a lot of family, and they would come up to see my games. There was a good piece of advice he gave me: "Just play your position, son. Don't worry about the big play, the crowd, or the awards." I never forgot that.

#16   Brent Ellis

SKIPPING CLASS

Those who rise fast can fall just as fast. I'm getting there slowly, and I'll make it to graduation without skipping any classes. Even if I'm held back, God will let me get to a new level. I'm thankful to Him for holding on to me and never leaving me, even when it looked like He wasn't there. He is always there. If He is here with me, even the setbacks are progress.

I never had much interest in school, but I had to maintain a good GPA to be eligible to get on the field, so I held it together during the season. But when I wasn't playing football, I found other things to keep my interest, and it wasn't school. When I was a high schooler, they had a system that would call your home and leave a recorded message when your child wasn't in school that day. But I was slick in my own way; I figured how to beat the system. I knew they checked only the first period, so I made sure to always make that first period—that way, I would get credit for being in attendance. Today, they report every period—they have to—so my system wouldn't work, ha ha. So once I was counted, we (me and my homeboys) would leave and do our thing—as long as we weren't pulled by police, because they would take truant kids to the detention center, which was near the armory. That's when they called your parents and had them come pick you up. We really didn't cause any trouble. We just weren't where we were supposed to be. But we were adolescents growing up and seeing what the world was all about.

Skipping class was no good, and it still isn't. Yes, it was the best fun then, but I should have been in school. I missed important stuff, and it didn't serve me well with my grades or help in preparation for college. The reality of it is that sometimes we make stupid choices when we're young. Yeah, it was fun, and it was all about exploring life, but skipping classes to go have fun with friends is never the best choice.

As I continued going through my teen years and the stages of becoming a man, I started doing things that were also not good choices. I went to the streets—of course, not all the way, but I was beginning to grow up a li'l' too fast. I wanted money, and I never liked asking my parents because I was raised to be independent. So at fifteen years old, I got my first job at a car wash. I was putting money in my pocket, but at the same time, I was meeting different people and getting introduced to different things and different ways to make money. It wasn't long before I started getting my hands dirty.

I was dabbling in the streets, but I never liked guns, so using them wasn't part of finding my way. I saw the effects of guns from both sides, the shooter and the victim, how the families of both were affected, so I didn't rob anybody or fight with guns, but I learned ways to defend myself. Once when I was skipping school, we got into a big fight at the beach. It was between us and those from another school. I don't really remember how the fight started, but when you mix kids with drugs and alcohol, something is usually going to happen. We all know how drugs can destroy families, how they can destroy the body, and I knew all this, but I was finding my own way, so I first smoked weed when I was skipping class, going to places like the beach. There we were, drinking, smoking weed, and fighting. Nobody ever knew how the fighting started, but I remember one time just mentioning my school was mixed and there were some racial issues. Before you know it, there was a big race war, a brawl, basically black against white. I didn't have a gun, and nobody else did either, just rocks, bats, feet, and hands. Finally, the police had to come out because there were lots of us and it caused a scene.

There was even more going on around this time. There were spots like Pac Jam and Heart of the City, where we would hang out. We also found our way into a few strip clubs. But despite my finding my way, I always knew that my parents expected me to graduate from high school. A lot of parents today aren't as involved as they should be in the things their children do, in or out of the home. While growing up, I had no privacy—no locked bedroom door at any time. My parents had a free pass to look through my room and see what was going on. That probably made all the difference because I knew I had to respect home. I knew my mom could see the change in me and knew I was getting involved in things because I started getting home later and later at night. But she let me grow up and find my way all the time, knowing God had His hands on me.

These days, things are different. Children are more expressive and seem to say anything to their parents. I've even noticed on church grounds how little respect they have. Of course, we did our thing growing up, and I did my thing in the streets, but respect for my elders and church grounds were always a must for me. I'm not sure if the laws today put too many restrictions on parents and how they raise their kids in their own homes, but I do know that home is the foundation and it needs to be solid. Remember: the home affects the neighborhood, which affects the community, and which eventually affects the whole nation. The man is the head of the family, but he has to be careful not to allow anything to destroy the seeds because that kills off the future. Kill the head, and eventually, the body will fall. If we don't take control of our kids, if we're not disciplining our kids, then we lose hold of them and the the law disciplines them for us.

Nobody is responsible for raising our children but us, the parents. Our children have been given to us by God, for us to raise and teach them the way. They are on loan to us here on earth. Even our lives aren't our own; our money, homes, clothes, cars, jobs, gifts, and talents we bring to a marriage are not ours. We and all we possess belong to God. All these things are blessings that help us get through life so that we can glorify Him. The Lord gives and takes away, and no matter what comes and goes, we need to bless His name, as all blessings come from Him. Too often, people receive the blessings and forget. They hold their things higher than the one who gave them and begin to worship the things that are created when they should be worshiping the creator.

WHAT I DO KNOW

ork can be very demanding, but we have to keep in mind that a job is just a job—no more than that. It's not your whole life. Not even if it's one that promises a career. It's not your whole life. You can't have your life revolve around a job, because they come and go. Our lives are bigger than the things we obtain in our lives. Ultimately, God is bigger than life because even that can be taken away at any moment, which is why it's not good to pursue riches only. Success is not measured by our riches and how much money we have. Things that this world gives us or that have a cost can always be replaced. We can make money and then turn around and lose it. Money does not bring success. Money comes as a result of having a successful state of mind and attitude, because success is doing what you believe in your heart you should be doing. We decide what success is by our own definitions, and the first thing we have to understand is that success is not something that money can buy.

I believe success is seeking and living to fulfill God's purpose for us because He will provide everything we need to live by His will. Positions, titles, status, and money should not be allowed to get to our heads. It's God who allows it to be in the first place, so when we let the things we have attained, achieved, and accomplished in this world control us, we put ourselves in a position to be manipulated by anything that comes along. It's important to always keep a level head and stay down to earth mentally. Never take yourself so seriously that you can't laugh at yourself. If we learn from our mistakes, it makes us able to get better at what we do and who we are, and we always want to grow in every level of our lives. It doesn't matter how much wisdom and experience we have—there's always something to learn from someone who may not have made it as far as we have. When we take ourselves too seriously and feel that we have arrived, we stop growing because we feel we've reached the pinnacle of our lives and we're above making mistakes. There's always room for growth, so the best thing is to build a solid foundation in Christ and stand on Him as our rock. When storms come to knock us down—and they will—we will still be standing.

Give all your desires, dreams, and goals to God because the enemy can manipulate even when you have a good motive. Remember the overall cause is more important than the individual gain because it's our individual contributions that we add to the overall cause. When our time for that season has passed for whatever we're doing, we've gotta get out the way and allow the next individuals to make their contributions. Just like seasons change every year, our lives are full of many different seasons, so many opportunities to transition from one point in life to the next.

When I got back from being away at college, everything was different. Things at home had drastically changed, and my mom was now living with her sister in Miami. She eventually went back to our house and started rebuilding her life, so I moved back in with her until I could get on my feet.

Little did I know things were about to take a turn for the worse for me. I hadn't earned my degree as planned, but while I was going to school, I learned a lot of lessons in life.

I started looking for work and had a lot of different jobs. I had never had any kind of skill or trade. Every man needs to have at least one skill under his belt that can earn him a living, even if he plans to get a college degree. Things don't always go as we planned. I had jobs from warehouse work, truck driving, construction, and concrete cleaning to cooking, lawn maintenance, and janitorial work. Basically, anything my experience and education would allow me to get, and whoever was hiring, I was willing to work, and I wasn't above day labor, which I did for a while. But it's hard to maintain a steady income when you're not on a stable job, so I lost job after job, sometimes because of my attitude. I seemed to always be angry with my financial situation, never having the bucks to enjoy anything. When you live in a tourist place like Florida, it's hard to see the rich and famous come and play right in your backyard when all you're doing is trying to keep your head up, which I did. As I write and reflect, I'm realizing how I never made excuses or blamed anyone for how things turned out in my life, but I'm also learning how important it is to study your choices and make the right ones.

Just as Florida is a tourist place, it's also a place that offers opportunities of almost any kind. By this, I mean that I had moved from mixing cocaine with weed in a joint to sniffing it straight to my head, and cocaine was everywhere. As this became more and more of a habit, it would finally lead to a steeper and steeper downward slope. Around this time, violence had risen, and in almost every party or club, there was shooting. I'm sure it had a lot to do with the areas where I was hanging.

I knew better. I had seen it too many times, too many people, too many generations, and I thought I was finding my own way, making my own path, but I was only going down the same destructive path others before me had gone. I didn't realize that I was going through what I thought was a necessary process—one I had to go through to get to where I am now—because I really was trying to do better. I just hadn't reached that point in my life that empowered me to do so.

Having odd jobs here and there left me with a lot of time on my hands. I never considered myself a dopeboy because I always kept a side hustle. I never wanted my money to come from one source. I'm the kind of person who if I want something done, I'll do it myself. I hadn't had a job for a few months, and day labor was getting old. It was like hustling just to get a job for the day. You had to get there very early and hope to get picked up for the day. It wasn't even guaranteed daily money, because some days you would get work and some days you wouldn't. Even though no one was hiring, and I was applying for a lot of different jobs, I still had to find ways to put money in my pocket.

We need to learn to be independent and create ways to make our money. Sometimes we can start a business or be blessed enough maybe to learn a family business. But that wasn't the case for me. My only option was a job at that point in my life. All I knew was having a job somewhere or hustlin' for it. I didn't have any trade or skill, so I was learning as I went along. Also, when I say *hustlin'*, it ain't nothin' but a term I use for "working hard for your money independently." Just to be clear, and out of respect for the many brothers who are out there hustlin' every day, just because someone says they are hustlin' doesn't mean they are doing things illegally. There are a lot of ways we can make money on our own for our families and our futures other than illegally. Everything's gotta start from somewhere, and when it's something that is real and you want it to last, it usually starts off slow. We have to have patience, because when it starts too fast, it can sometimes end just as fast.

You have to be careful not to get caught up in the chase for power, fame, fortune, and riches, because eventually, you're gonna come to a certain point where you can't go any further without giving up something of yourself; all those things come with a price. Nothing in the world is free. There are a lot of creative ways to make our own money if we humble ourselves enough to just live practically and comfortably.

As I was trying to keep my head above water, trying to understand the man I was growing to be, I was hustlin', but unfortunately, at this time in my life, the only form of hustlin' I was doing was illegal. So I started hustlin' with some dudes I met along the way who I didn't know too well because we weren't from the same area. I hadn't grown up with them, and I really had no business with these people like that around me. One thing about the game is that everything goes. It's very cutthroat, and it don't matter what level of game you playin'. Dudes in suits and ties from big corporations have game just as dirty—the game of cutthroat (distrust) and everything else goes.

My people, close friends I grew up and went to school with, were telling me to get those dudes from around me, but I was hardheaded. I remember a certain instance when I didn't see I had walked into an already heated situation, because the spot I was on had a lot of traffic, lots of people coming and going. One day, I was slipping and got caught myself. I can't really remember how it all went down, but basically the dudes I was with were stepping on somebody else's shoes round there. It was their bread and butter, and my clique was competition to their money. I was caught in the middle. There I was, and my life was about to change in a way I had never, ever experienced. I saw them surrounding me, so I started defending myself because I knew they were gonna jump me. Then I felt a brick hit me. It hit me so hard I ain't even know where it came from because I didn't see the dude in front of me swing. But I remember thinking, *I don't know how the hell I'm gonna fight this dude. I ain't never been punched this hard.* Turned out it wasn't a punch; it was a metal pipe. I got a good beatdown, but I remember thinking that I must not be unconscious or dead, because I heard "Kill dis nigga." I couldn't really see because blood was in my eyes, but I was expecting to hear a gunshot or something. It must not have been my time to go, because I'm still here. (All the slang used in certain areas is for effect; my purpose throughout is to give you a truer understanding of who I am.)

My head wasn't really in the right place, because I could smell my own blood. I had a gash behind my head with so much blood leaking from it that I felt like I was tasting it at that point. I was messed up, and all I was thinking about was getting a pistol so I could get rid of them—but I couldn't. There was no pistol in the house no more because Mama had had bad feelings with a gun in the house and later told me that she'd gotten rid of it. It had been her dad's gun, anyway, and her right to get it out. She didn't believe weapons protected us—God did. So it must have been by the grace of God that I didn't get my hands on that pistol or any other one that night.

God was looking out for me that night more than I ever knew. I know that now. I had a hole in my head, and instead of going to the hospital, I went around to a friend's house, smoking and drinking. When I finally got home, my mind was still on how I was going to get those dudes back. That is, until my mom saw me.

I had wiped up a lot of the blood, but she had heard from family what had happened. She came in from work—she taught classes at night—and when she saw me and all the blood on my shirt, she hit the floor crying. "Oh, Lord, my child. Please don't let me lose my son, my child. I'm gonna lose my son." This was real. This wasn't nothin' from no television program. This was a woman who had put everything she had into raising her child, her only child; a woman who had sacrificed so much and had been so strong for her son through some painful times of her own; a woman who had prayed for her son every day of her life; a woman who had basically willed her son back to reality on the day of his own son's funeral, prayed in him the will to get up off that hospital gurney and convinced him that his life wasn't over by speaking those encouraging words in his ear—the words that he had grown up with from the time he was a child. And there she was, on the ground, broken.

I had never seen her down and broken like that. She was always my life force. I had to take a seat for a second. It was so hard seeing her like that. Then I got up and tried to pick her up and comfort her, saying, "I'm OK, Ma. Look—I'm right here. I'm OK, Ma." It didn't work. Nothing worked. I was standing right there, but it didn't matter. She was hurting deep, and it's very hard to describe that experience in words. See, I didn't really care about myself no more, didn't really care about life because I felt life had taken away from me so much that was important. I had already seen my name in an obituary, so in my eyes, I had died when my son died. But when I saw how much my life affected my mom, I decided right then that I sho can't be on nobody's corner selling no dope no more. I have to be honest: it wasn't the last time I sold, but I never got back on the corner. Still, it was the start of things beginning to turn around.

CHANGE IS COMING

The bad thing is I had no money, no job—nothing but a pocketful of work, or drugs to sell. I had a new perspective, though, as I could be touched. I wasn't invincible, so that made me very alert and more aware of my surroundings. I would hit the corner store, get off what I could, and then keep it moving. Eventually, I got rid of the rest of the work, but I was still dealing with my own substance-abuse problem staring me in the face, waiting to be confronted.

I was beginning to feel like I was really cursed or something. My name line was doomed; my dad used to say it was like the men in our family were cursed. Cursed? I'd never understood that, but from the way things had gone up to that point, it seemed that way. My dad was the only male survivor of our name line. His dad had had all kinds of issues but had died a while before; his only brother, with same name as his father, had died young from drowning; my only son was dead; a male family member I loved and respected had been shot and killed tragically right in his driveway; and here I was on the same path of men before me with serious issues—but I was determined now to end this so-called Ellis curse.

A time for change had come. My dad had a place in Miami, so

I went to stay with him to get some guidance. Even though I was really dealing with some challenges, I gotta be honest: I felt blessed that I never went through what my dad had gone through. He did say something during that time that stuck with me to this day, though. I was about nineteen, and he said to me, "You know your life is going in a downward spiral, right?" I gave him a confused look but said, "Yeah, I know." Then, a few minutes later, he said, "You're going to break the generational curse." Man, that was such a light to me. He just didn't know how much I needed to hear that, and even though I didn't quite understand that curse thing, I felt encouraged that he believed in me—like he was depending on me, passing me the baton.

After I told him things weren't going good in my life and I asked him in what direction I was supposed to go, he told me, "Ask God what His will is for your life." That one stuck with me the most. In fact, before I do anything or make any major decisions, almost every day of my life, that's my prayer. We were bonding again, and I had my friend back, the main man I respected so much. He wasn't at his best during these times, and I'm sure he'd be the first to say so, but there's always room for us all to do better. All I cared about was that he was my father and I loved him.

So now I was staying with my dad because obviously I needed him. I was looking and reaching for anything that would stick. It was his suggestion that I come and stay with him. The whole plan was for me to get a steady job. Pops made sure I ate every day, and he would wake up early each day and take me to waste management, where I'd try to get on with one of the truck drivers as a helper. It was just like day labor: you had to be there early and wait for work, but for drivers, it was all about seniority; they took only the guys they had already worked with. So I was out—kept going every day but never got work.

I finally suggested he take me to Labor Ready and see if I could get some work there, but it was same thing, the same results. I felt that if a man didn't work, he didn't eat. My cousin was living not too far away, so he would come pick me up sometimes to get me out of the house. One thing I love about my cousins: they never judged me. They always accepted me as I was, and still do, and whenever I called, they were there. They never were a bad influence on me. They just let me be a part of whatever they were doing whenever I reached out to them. My other cousin was up the road getting a college degree, making family history as first male in our family to get his master's. But all three of my cousins have been the first ever to do something great. I don't have to say names, because they know who they are, but I love y'all, man.

So my cous' and I were chillin' daily. Sometimes we'd be in a trap. Our hands were clean, but that was the only life we knew. I was spending a lot of time with my dad too, bonding with him like we never had before, talking, listening to music and sermons. Even though I thought I had found my way, I was still listening to, looking to, respecting, and following my dad. I was getting past the anger and the image I had built up because of certain situations we'd dealt with as a family. We were making our peace, a phase that every father and son needs to have. We were talking about struggles we'd had to overcome, women, drugs, sports, and we talked a lot about God. I was very thankful because so many I knew didn't have their dads in their lives at all, so this was all good.

In my mind, it was like a second chance for catching up with all we had missed—time for renewing our bond. I didn't think my dad felt there ever was anything missing between us, and I think that's because most men feel that as long as they are still providing and they haven't left the family, then things should be good. But to a son, to a child during those growing years, quality time is all he wants and needs from his father. "I'm getting my son on the right track" was what he said to everyone he talked to, and that felt good to me, because he seemed proud to be helping me and I was glad to be getting help from him through the Lord. I was looking at everything, and my dad's words were like gold to me.

One night, my dad and I were going home from a cousin's wedding reception, and he spoke real hard truth with me by sharing for the first time how he had overcome his demons. He talked about ones of his past that he had battled and conquered. I felt proud. Hearing who he was and what he had to battle meant more to me than anything had in a long time, and what meant even more was that, for the first time, he was telling it to me. I was hearing it directly from him. A son wants to be his dad's best friend—at least that's what I want to be to my sons—so if there's something about me that they should know, it's important our bond is such that they get it straight from me. This time, I was hearing who my dad was straight from him—not from cousins or other family members. I really felt whole for a change. My dad was talking to me, his only son, and confiding in me, and I can't tell you how important that was and how good it felt.

Not long after that night, the holidays were on us, and I'll never forget. It was Thanksgiving time, and my pops brought my uncle over so we could all go to my grandma's house the next day for Thanksgiving dinner. Even though I was still getting my mental stimulation at times, I had stopped a lot of my bad habits while staying with my pops, so I was OK with just sitting around, chillin' with my uncle. We were talking, relating about everything, and having fun, with nothing stronger than a few cold ones.

That was a good feeling, just thinking about the day ahead. It was going to be my first Thanksgiving with that part of my family in a long time, and then to be with my dad—this was going to be a good day. My uncle and I really had a great time that night, and I'm glad that I always try to celebrate the moment I'm in, because sometimes things don't always go as planned. This was one of those times. My uncle wanted to wait with me, but I told him to go ahead. I figured I would see him later.

Well, you may have already guessed, but I didn't get to that Thanksgiving dinner as planned. It was a real disappointment. Thankfully, Mom, being Mom, called to wish us all a good day, but she soon realized from my tone that something wasn't good. I didn't want to talk about it, and she didn't ask, so I asked her to come pick me up. But I surely didn't want to be dropped at the family dinner and have to sit at the table and hear "I told you," so I was back home for Thanksgiving with Mom, which was always good. Even though it wasn't where I thought I would be, I learned something very important. I learned that a battle doesn't have to be finished to be a lesson; you don't have to be done, and it doesn't have to be won in order for you to help somebody else. I was needing help, and I got it from my dad during a time when he was still dealing with his own issues. I was ready for truth—or whatever we shared, so long as it was real, and I felt it was. Truth can solidify so much between a father and his son. It enhances the lessons he teaches him. I believed I had found my truth—the truth that my experience on that day and my time with him gave me, the truth he wanted for me. That truth was to learn from his mistakes, and even though he never really said it, I felt that's what he wanted me to take away from that time I spent with him. I think he knew and felt it was the best lesson he could've given me. It turned out he was right.

MOVING ON

My cousin's mom, my aunt, knew of a trade school for a heavy-equipment license, except it was in New York. She called her sister, our aunt in New Jersey, close to where the school was located, and she was on board, so my cousin and I now had plans, having been invited to live with her until we finished the course. Man, I was so excited and ready for this opportunity, but when I got up there, Auntie changed her mind and said that I couldn't stay there. Now, this was an aunt on my father's side, but my mom also had a sister up there, and she was the one who'd initially picked me up from the station and taken me to the house of my aunt who lived closer to the school and was the main reason we had plans to stay there.

When my aunt Charlotte and I got there, we were turned around at her door, bags in hand. Thanks to my aunt, because without her, I truly would have had nowhere to go! You can imagine how that felt, especially with no warning. Before we'd left to go up, my cous' and I had done everything my aunt had asked in order for us to stay with her. One of the main things was to cut our dreads. We did. She didn't want anyone with dreads living in her house, and I didn't care what I had to sacrifice—I was hungry for something and needed this training.

I thought I had cleared everything with her. I'd spoken to her directly before going up there, and she told me with confidence that if I cut my hair, I could come and get into school. So I was ready. But plans changed. I understood—she had two daughters living at home then, and my cous' had gotten there not too long before me, so I guess she felt having me there, too, was a li'l' too much. There were no hard feelings. Again, there's that li'l' thing called *truth*. It would have been so much better had I been told before that she wasn't planning to let me stay there, especially after I'd made all the changes and spent so much money just to get up there.

NO TURNING BACK

I wasn't going to turn back, not now. My feeling was that I was up there and had to make this thing work. I was thankful at least that my mom's sister was there and didn't mind me staying with her. My cous' and I went through our necessary steps—got jobs, went to all the places we needed to go to get proof of residency and assistance to qualify for school. There we were, all the paperwork in place, so we hopped on the subway looking forward to meeting the lady who owned the school.

We got to the appointment on time and were more than excited. When we finally met the head of the school, it was a completely different setup from what we'd been told. We'd sent the necessary fees, which weren't cheap; thankfully, my mom had taken care of that. She'd also spent several hundred dollars on a full winter wardrobe for me. Everything was all systems go. Sometimes things that happen to us are not always on us; sometimes they happen as a result of other people's actions, which can affect our choices. So there we were, literally standing there, prepared and eager to get started— and remember school was never my favorite place, but I was ready this time—only to find out, according to this lady, that we weren't eligible to get into the school. No reason given. We also found out that the school might not have been fully accredited. At that point, it was questionable, and we were wondering if it had been a scam from the very beginning. No money was ever refunded. Apparently, they were protected, and no further explanation was given.

One day, my cous' told me that when came home from work, our aunt sent him away too, telling him he couldn't stay there anymore. So now we were both up a creek. We'd gone up there with good intentions and done everything the way we were supposed to, but things didn't go our way. I was very disappointed, but that's life—another lesson learned.

Things don't always go the way we expect. Sometimes it's what we do, and as I said earlier, sometimes it's what other people do. We can't control what others do or the things that happen to us; all we can control is ourselves and how we handle what comes at us. We was handlin' it the best we could. We were used to things going wrong. Good thing my other aunt let us come stay with her. She's a good soul.

We were able to find jobs, but that's not the reason we were there. We were supposed to be attending school, starting over, learning a trade, and getting certified for a lifelong career. Instead, we were doing the same thing we had been doing at home, just working. But we made the best of it. We just took the opportunity of working up there as one to get to see New York. We would get on transit and walk around Harlem, down Lennox and 125th Street, and we saw the Apollo, ate soul food at the famous Sylvia's Restaurant, saw all the shops in fast-paced New York, and even witnessed a shakedown by New York undercover. It was all a new experience for me, because up to that point, all I knew was Miami. I hadn't traveled outside Florida much except for the Bahamas with my family and to Tennessee to visit my cousin up in college.

One thing I noticed about people in New York is that they seem to love people from down here. I stood out like a sore thumb because of my accent, my clothes—my whole style was different. But the entire time we were up there, we had no problems because that was our vibe. It doesn't matter where you are from. It's who you are and how you carry yourself. We knew the streets enough to not be rookies; we knew how to handle ours and stay out of anybody else's lane.

We met a lot of people and did and saw a lot, and for the first time, I saw snow! After a few months passed, it was time to go back to South Florida—unfortunately without a new career but fo' sho with a lot of new experiences. Ain't that what life's all about?

Some people would like to be an egg with a shell of hardness as their protection. Personally, I strive to be like coffee beans. When coffee beans are put in boiling water, they don't change their form in the way that an egg or a carrot does; an egg turns hard inside, and the carrot turns soft, but coffee beans mix in water and change the color of the water. So don't let nothin' change who you are inside. When we go through the fire, the adversities and challenges of life, it makes us cold and hard, broken down, or soft and wilted—or it changes us and brings out the best in us and others. When we stand our ground and, in turn, change things around us, there's an opportunity to make an impact on our world instead of the world changing us.

I saw this to be so true when I got back home. Even though I picked up my old habit, it never changed who I was inside. I noticed that any time we return to something we left behind, it's even harder to stop the second time around. It seems that in its absence, it gains strength. I realized that when we change our environment even for a short while, it don't matter where we go—we gotta take ourselves wit' us. And if we don't know who we are inside, we may change ourselves, but we bring the same issues wit' us.

STRONG BLOODLINES

A ll my cousins had their own talents. One of them had the gift of athleticism, playing baseball, and he also cut hair. My other cousin had the gift of intelligence—he is very smart. They both had enough talent to be anything they wanted to be, but while circumstances may not have allowed them to play in the major leagues, own a barber shop, or become a math professor or an innovator of science and medical research and technology, I'm proud to say they all grew to be great fathers. They're good to their families and making an honest living. We often become the products of our environment—products of where we are from—and Miami was our environment. We know that as a people, we are not always offered the same opportunities as others who don't look like us and who have less talent and skills. And that's no excuse. That's just fact.

As for me, I met a young lady shortly after I got back to South Florida, and we got involved and had a son. He was born December 9, 2002. Coincidentally, it was the same day that, twenty-seven years before, my mom lost her mother. Naturally, for years, until my son's birth, that date left her with a bad memory and an emptiness, as I'm sure it would for anyone who lost a loved one. You can prepare yourself emotionally each year that date rolls around, but you're still never prepared for how it affects you, so it was like God gave her a gift when my son was born. Now, instead of that day being filled with sadness due to a loss, it became a day to celebrate the birth of a grandchild. So he was here and healthy and a blessing after the loss of my first son. I spent a lot of time with him, and I remember him being so small I would bathe him in the bathroom sink. His mother and I got along well even though we didn't stay together. We shared time with him. As time went on, I started having him most of the time, until she eventually decided to let him come live with me permanently. I will always love and respect her for that.

I know that mothers are special—they are the best, and they are strong—but I always feel it's important for boys to have as much input from their fathers, when possible. Of course, mothers want their babies with them, and my son's mother felt the same way. I was just so fortunate that this mother allowed this father to raise their son. Some mothers take pride in situations in which their children's fathers are in the children's lives because they want to be, not because they are ordered by the state, which, in turn, through child support, paints that involved father as a deadbeat. This sends the wrong message. But thank God for those who realize that no matter who has the children full-time, children should not be used like pawns to sow discord in failed relationships or looked at as a means for additional income. This was not the case with his mother.

My son has been with me since he was six months old. I take pride in being a father, and I take it very seriously. Along with my mom's motherly help and nurturing, her wisdom, and her affectionately looking over my shoulder, I became a full-time father.

At the start, I was raising my son at my mom's, but I was responsible for fully supporting him, so I needed more than just a job. I needed a career, so I got into trade school for cooking and earned a certificate. It took a while, but I finally landed a job as a cook. Everywhere I went, he went. When he wasn't in day care, he was with me. I changed diapers, stayed up at night when he was sick, fed him—the whole nine. We had him christened at my great-grandparents' church in Miami, and two of my cousins stood as godfathers. I felt that if anything happened to me, I had two people who knew me from day one and whom I knew would show my boy the right things about life.

It was at this time that I felt I should try again to get my college degree in order to secure a better, more stable income, so I started at the University of Phoenix. My plate was full. While I was taking online classes part-time, I was working as a cook, keeping money in my pocket and enjoying taking care of my li'l' boy. It seemed that, finally, things were looking positive and I was on the way to finishing what I had started several years before. I would get the rest of my college credits and ultimately get my college degree. My grades were looking good, and I felt confident. Sounded like a winning plan, right? Although taking classes online, rather than sitting in classes all day, had its advantages, eventually the day came that I had to stop. Aside from the challenge of finishing what I had started, there were other challenges I hadn't resolved. So the problem from before was still there—I had no degree—but now I had college loans and was dealing with a substance-abuse problem.

Before my son was living with me permanently, as I said earlier, I was living a different kind of life, except now I was playing the hokeypokey with it, one foot in, one foot out. I left the door open without ever confronting it, and any time we leave a door open, no matter how big or small the opening, it's always enough room for the enemy to creep back. My problem was still there. It had me in places and with people I had no business being around. I was blessed to have my mom around so much because even though I always came home, I was able to do my thing in the streets and never bring it around my son. Plenty of times, I would wake up the next day, at home, not knowing how I'd even gotten there from the night before.

I remember one night I was out with my homeboys doing what we did, drinking, drugging, everything. I should have just crashed at my homeboy's house and waited to drive home the next day, but I decided to drive home that night. I was so messed up that all I remembered later was getting on the expressway. Next thing I remembered was my mom waking me up. I was sitting in my car, parked on the swale, with my keys still in the ignition. I must have been asleep the whole time I was driving. Thank God no one was hurt by my carelessness, and thank God for watching over me that night.

Well, those of us who have been there understand that it wasn't me driving that car; it was simply God's grace and mercy. I had seen enough of everything, and the one thing I know about overcoming bad habits is that they have a strong hold on us. We're not gonna get them out of our lives till we're ready and completely tired of living that way.

I was tired of living that way, tired of myself, tired of getting nowhere, and tired of the same ol' thing. Out of all the things I did in my life, I never went to jail, except for minor traffic violations—suspended license but no felonies. I went to jail the first time because of child support. The other time was when the Broward Sheriff's Office (BSO) came to the house at six in the morning to pick me up for a bench warrant. They even came before my deadline to pay, according to the information online, and even though my mom had a legal document proving that I was not in violation of the court date and actually showed it to them, they didn't care 'bout' no computer foul-up, which had caused the order for the arrest to be issued. It was obvious they needed to fill their quota.

Mom bonded me out later, but I was out with all these repercussions. I guess my past was finally catching up with me.

Prisons are built, and since they don't get money unless they have warm bodies in the beds, they've gotta keep them filled. Unfortunately, mostly young black men are filling those prison cells. I believe they twist the law in a lot of situations to where they can throw men in jails made for real criminal offenders, and unfortunately, black men get the most of this. I know from experience that they'll throw a man in jail for civil matters like nonpayment of child support, sometimes in the same cell with men waiting to do hard time.

I also believe that the system makes more money this way—it's like a domino effect. You go to jail, your driver's license is suspended when you get out, you've gotta go to court to get it back because you need it to drive to find a job, and now you've got court fees, which you can't pay because you lost your job, so, again, you can't pay child support and the cycle repeats itself. So you go back to jail, and now you're back with hard-core criminals. It's the system—yes, it's broken, and it has always been—but it's also a business. It's about money and often built on the backs of men and women trying to find their way after having made bad choices. I'm not making excuses for anyone who breaks the law, but there needs to be something put in place for those who are doing time for noncriminal behavior. In other words, child support laws need to be reviewed.

TAKING DEFINING STEPS

F irst thing I had to do was confront this demon, and to do that, I had to accept that I had one and kill it before it killed me and everyone around me. I put myself in a Narcotics Anonymous program. I didn't make any announcements, because I didn't have to. I wasn't court ordered as a result of drug-trafficking charges or possession of illegal drugs—nothing like that. I went because I wanted to change my life. I met a lot of people and learned a lot by going to those meetings, and it helped a lot, but something was missing.

Twelve-step programs are very effective, but they give credit for overcoming your problem to a higher source—"a god of my understanding" is what they called it. All my life, the god of my understanding and higher source had a name: I knew Him as Christ. Don't know what you call Him, or who your source is, but for me, Christ, the anointed one and son of God, was mine.

I was doing well and had been clean for about six months—no drugs, no alcohol—and everything was going good until, one day, I went to a parent-teacher meeting at my son's school. I was the only father present in my kid's class. Afterward, I dropped my son off at his mom's, so I was on my own time. I was feeling myself a li'l' too much, though. I had a decent job that provided insurance and paid vacations, something I'd never had before, and I was getting raises every six months with good evaluations. I was feeling good about myself. I had been clean, and I was providing for my son and heavily involved in his life. Everything was good, so I talked myself into believing that I deserved to treat myself when I should've stopped to think that all the credit for any of my good belonged to God.

It just so happened that my son's school was just around the corner from the spot I used to go to for my stuff, so I listened to the enemy in my ear, telling me to go ahead and get a bag of that white stuff. *It won't hurt nothin'*, I told myself. *It's just one bag. That's all. You deserve it, Brent, and now you're strong enough—you can use a little and still control it.* I gave in to temptation and went there. Once again, God stepped in and said no. Right after I pulled up, I walked to the door, and two BSO officers pulled up also. I had to think quick, so I acted like I was just stopping by to see a friend because I knew if I had bought that bag, I would've gotten pulled, and they would've found the bag and taken me back to jail, this time on a stronger charge. I would've lost my license and my job, and most of all, I would've lost my son. I hopped back in my car, drove off, and never looked back. That was the last time I had any episode with that substance. Right then, I made a commitment. I didn't use it anymore, didn't sell it, and didn't touch it. All by the grace of God.

All before this commitment, I had been in several situations in which I had been pulled with drugs on me. One night, while out with friends, I had about an ounce under my seat, but it was balled up like trash, and the police somehow never saw it. I'm sure they knew what we were up to because of the time and the area, so they pulled us over but didn't find any evidence. Thank God they didn't call the dogs. When I was in front of that trap, when the police pulled up, I was fearful of losing my freedom, but still, it didn't end there. Another time, when I was just as foolish, one Friday night, I had gotten a "fourteen," and by Sunday morning, it was all gone. I had gone through a whole half ounce by myself. I remember some nights being up all night long, snortin' and bustin' licks. That's when you're delivering the substance as the customers call and still making it to work right after bustin' your last lick thirty minutes prior.

Although this happened years ago, each incident had a great impact on my life, and I can never forget how much God carried me when I couldn't carry myself. I'm thankful that I changed. As I said, I love being a father and wouldn't want to live with the thought of losing my freedom or losing the opportunity to raise my son.

In those early years, when my son was with me, he was mostly with my mom during the week—that way, I never jeopardized his safety any time he was with me. My mom dropped him to school because I had to be at work too early and his school wasn't open at that time. So as much as I would have liked, it didn't work for me to take him. The arrangement was for me to have him on weekends, when he was my only concern, my only business—no drugs, no drug activity, he had all my attention. I spent quality time with him.

I knew if I had gone to jail for anything that night, I would have lost him for good, so that night woke me up. It's like God had spoken to me again—once through my mom to save my life, now through my five-year-old son—and I listened. Finally, victory! I had overcome my addiction and substance-abuse problem. Glory be to God!

In the middle of all this, I finally had my own place, and I met a young lady who was close to my family. We became heavily involved, and yes, we had a child. So now I had my second son. Having fully recovered from substance abuse, with two boys, and a young woman living with me, I now had a family. I had my day job and a part-time night job. I started to wise up and started thinking about a future for my kids. I needed to establish something to pass down to my kids—something from which they could hopefully benefit—so they could somehow learn from what I'd built and use it to realize the value of working for themselves and not for another person. So I took advantage of things I was learning from my day job, thinking, *I'm working for a cooperation, making them richer and richer, when I can take what I'm learning, flip it, and start making money for me and mine.*

I bought some small equipment and started doing lawns on the side, for a few reasons. The first was to make a better life for my family—my lady and children—so their futures would be more secure. The second was to be in a position to provide work for the younger men in my immediate family. That way, if ever they needed it, or at any time couldn't find employment, they would always have the means to make a dollar. I figured they could always come and work with me, get paid while learning a skill, and maybe branch off and do their own thing. If we're not living for our purpose, there's no purpose in living.

Every man has a duty, a reason why God created him and put him here. We're driven by our purpose, and when a man has no purpose, he dies inside. If there's no solid reason behind what he's doing, he'll begin to feel all his work is being done in vain, for no reason, like he's just waking up every day and going through the motions of working, paying the bills, and so on—going through the drudgery of life. When we don't have a purpose, our actions are not precise and accurate, because they're not focused on where we're going and other things easily distract us. When we know our purpose, we can focus all our energy and effort on it. When we reach a certain level of maturity, we begin to put things into perspective; our priorities are in order: God, family, the way we make a living, and then of course education, if young children are involved.

There I was with a family, and all I wanted to do was please God, protect and provide, give love to my family, and be the best father I could be to my children. I always wanted to be a good example and help them be the best men they could be. I wanted to prepare a way for them, to somewhat be that launchpad to a good start so that they could avoid the struggles I'd endured. They redefined my journey.

I had a li'l' one-bedroom apartment on the east side of Fort Lauderdale, zip code 33311, an area concentrated with every device designed by the enemy to distract and destroy, but it was all my budget would allow, and like I said, it's about not where we are but who we are inside. No coincidence that this was a predominantly black neighborhood with a mix of those in poverty and hardworking people, like me, who weren't expecting or accepting nothin' from the government. But still, where there's poverty, crime usually follows. This was an area where drug use was heavy, along with teenage pregnancy, murders, sexual-identity confusion, single-parent homes, inequality in education—anything and everything you can think of in this area. So naturally, police were always around.

I remember during one short period of time, there were several— at least five or more—different instances where the news reported the shooting and killing of an unarmed black man by the police. Looking back, I also remember getting pulled by police, and they could pull you at any time, search and seize your possessions without a proper warrant, no probable cause other than being a black man in a high-drug-activity neighborhood. I started growing my hair back, and that only brought extra attention my way. Plenty of times, I got pulled for no reason at all. I remember one time they got behind me—it was undercover, the "jump-out" boys. I had my work uniform on and lawn equipment with me, but no matter, they still went through with their procedure. Put me on the ground, searched my car, called the dogs, and treated me like a criminal. Of course, they found nothing, because I was a man who worked for a living.

Another time, I had my son with me, sleeping in the car. They came and shined a light in my son's face, a cop on either side of the vehicle, their guns drawn. It felt like they hoped I would make one wrong move.

Then there was the time when I was coaching Little League football, dropping kids off after practice. I had a van by this time, and it was full of work equipment. They called the dogs and made me get out and sit on the curb in handcuffs while they searched my ride. I told them just what I was doing, but they didn't care. All that dog did was get his nose burned from the gasoline fumes from my equipment, ha ha.

In none of these instances was I doing anything wrong. I truly felt that this was all done because I was a black man with locks in a black community riddled with crime. I guess you might say, "What did you expect? That automatically makes you look suspicious," *but it shouldn't.* I understand they've gotta check you out because they're policing the neighborhood and don't know you from Adam, but why with such disrespect and degradation, in front of li'l' brothers who look up to you, like your son—in my case, members of my football team? Why is it necessary to automatically assume I did something wrong and that I don't deserve any respect because I am black and live in a certain community?

But I was thankful for peace of mind—that peace that passes through all understanding. You see, others didn't know what all I had been through, and it felt good for a change not being on the wrong side of the law. There was no better or more satisfying feeling than having the law pull me, hoping to find dope, and come away wit' nothin'. The peace I had when they pulled me and I didn't have to shuffle and move this stash here, move that one over there, making sure nothin' was out in the open. A lot of people may never know what I've been through and what that felt like, but my God knew. He is God of peace.

I felt good and was working a day job and a part-time job at night and starting a lawn business out of the trunk of my car— literally. I had a four-door Chevy Malibu. I was determined, and I had to be creative, so I would put my blower, string trimmer, and edger in back passenger seat and roll the window down so they would stick out the car a bit; that was the only way they would fit. My lawn mower was folded up in the trunk of the car, and I shaped a piece of plywood to use as my lift. I didn't have a truck or van yet—couldn't afford one—but I had the drive and desire to work, so I used what I had.

Once again, I was starting something new, so I had to build up customers and do the groundwork to get it started. So I printed out cards and flyers, and with my past, I had the know-how to sell what I was trying to do. I flooded the streets with ads for my lawn business, leaving them on cars and in grocery stores and Laundromats, even going door-to-door, meeting people and letting them know I had a lawn business.

I got my first customer from a friend at my day job. Family, I can't tell you what that did for me! I was now a business owner, and it felt good! After a while, my business was advertising itself by word of mouth, which is the best kind of advertisement.

I kept my day job with the company, which wasn't rocket science—just cutting grass, which called for a lot of walking in very hot weather. It was midsummer, and I was on one of the busiest routes at the job, Broward Boulevard. This route went from State Road 7 (known as 441) all the way down past Sawgrass Mall, to the end of Broward Boulevard. I didn't even know Broward Boulevard actually ended, ha ha. At least that's the way my body felt so many days after walking it up and down. My crew leader would say, "Get Weed eater, and keep walking"—walking miles in the hot sun, with the string trimmer on your shoulder, looking out for traffic in the middle of summer. After a day like that, I would get in my car and go do my lawns. Pullin' that lawn mower out of the trunk of my car, man! It was really taking a toll on my body. Determination. That's what kept me going. Doing this kind of manual labor takes its toll on a man. Sometimes it feels like a life sentence because it sure can take a piece out of your body. My back was locking up, and I got kidney stones and developed bone spurs on my feet from an old injury. My ankle had had an accident with a forklift. Seriously, it had happened years before on another job, and this kind of work brought it back with a vengeance. But I couldn't take any breaks, because my body was my means of making a living, my hands and my feet. So as I went, so did my way of providing a living for my family.

"God is a new beginning. Yesterday was exhausting, and I'll be exhausted again today. That sun is hot, and it's part of the territory, but every day is a new beginning. God gives me that new beginning every day. With new abilities, I wake up every morning and praise Him so I can be refreshed when the sun comes up, because God resets our days as if yesterday never existed." These words came from a deep place and reflected a long, long hard day, because so many times, writing was my only solace.

My business was picking up more and more, so I decided to quit the night job and dedicate more time and weekends to my family and business. But since I had done well and made an impact at my day job, the people there wanted me to stay. There was this very nice elderly sister who had a decent position and oversaw payroll. She suggested that instead of leaving, I trim down my schedule, stay on the payroll, and maybe work just one night. I had shared with her what I was trying to do with my business. She was a very down-to-earth person, sort of reminded you of one of those neighbors on your street who you called Auntie or some affectionate name like that. I was fully in drive mode, very determined, so I guess she saw that. I thanked her but resigned anyway. It's important to always give your all to whatever it is you do, to whatever task you undertake, and I was glad I did that there.

So with the business doing well, I was doing right by my family; I was able to bring my cousin along to help me. Actually, we helped each other, because we were both putting money in our pockets and I was fulfilling one of my goals, which was working with a family member to be a part of his making a few dollars. It turned out good because he was bringing new business and would always be with me when I had jobs in Miami.

There were times when we would hit it from sunup up to sundown, cutting ten to twelve lawns a day, all with a push mower in the middle of summer. At one point, I had a forty-account business, and money was coming in pretty good—and I needed every bit of it because my oldest son was living with me for the most part now, sometimes going back and forth to his grandma's house. I also had a newborn, so everything I was doing was definitely needed. This is the part of my journey that became the eye-opener for everything else to come.

RELATIONSHIPS

It's very important for two people to be on the same page when deciding to bring a child into the world, or things just don't go right. Without a plan, things just kind of ... go. A lot is misunderstood, especially if two people are not together on some level mentally or spiritually. If you don't at least have that, then you're in the relationship for the wrong reasons.

Relationships are hard. They call for each person to be responsible for what they bring to it and what they do for the good or bad of that relationship.

Many of us have gone through troubled times, and it's during those times that we look to family and friends for love and support. During such times, you might not seem like yourself, might not seem like the person they've always known, but the wholeness of a person doesn't change—sometimes it's just covered by things they are facing at the time. That was me at one time, but one thing's for sure: no matter how family or friends may have seen me at any given time during those troubled years, those years of trying to hold my family together, nobody could have ever said that I didn't stand up to my responsibilities. I took the blows and admitted my wrongs, and they could never say I didn't take care of my children. I'm not bragging or looking for anything extra for that, but everything I do is for my children because I know that everything I do or don't do affects them; every decision I make affects them, one way or the other, whether my love relationship is in harmony or not.

In relationships, you can't make excuses for your actions. I neither made excuses for mine nor hid behind other things. I was dealing with consequences that had resulted from my choices. But every mistake deserves just as much forgiveness, so as my journey continued, I was beginning to see more clearly.

Sometimes, during some of the toughest times in your life, some of the most important people in your life don't show up or give you understanding. These are people who know you. Sometimes you just take for granted the people who you feel should know the kind of man you are, who would stand up for you and represent you. Maybe I'm different, but with me, any time there is a question of who gets my loyalty, no matter the situation, I'm gonna always go with blood.

My character was being attacked, and any memory of my integrity was dismissed. Thank God for those cousins I grew up with, the ones I speak of throughout this book, my brothers—we always stuck together. My aunts on both my mom's and dad's sides had basically raised me, so they knew who I was, as well as of course my mom, grandma, and dad and other loyal family members who didn't care what others said or what mistakes I had made. They loved me unconditionally and knew I had a good heart and was a good person and good father. They knew I wanted the best for the people around me. I just wanted to be happy and see others happy, so I accepted people for who they were. I know that life is full of many choices, many decisions, and we don't always make the right ones, so it leads to mistakes. But for sure, we *all* have made them.

I learned early to forgive because God has forgiven me for so many things, but believe me—I trust my instincts and know my heart, and a lot has been done that's been hard to forgive. These were the times when this journey of mine became very rocky, but as much as I have done in my life, God has forgiven it all, so who am I not to do the same?

I had come to the point in my life where I welcomed adversity because it only made me stronger. Like a friend of mine once told me, "If God brought me to it, He gon' bring me through it." The relationship didn't last. It was turmoil from the start—all the ugly words and slanderous attacks that, having had bigger things to worry about, I kept to myself because I had to keep it movin'. We tried and tried and *tried* again! When you put yourself into trying to make something work, trying to maintain a mutual respect for the sake of children, trying to hold it together and stay together as a family, after a while, you have to let it go and realize it just ain't meant to be. So we moved on.

Beyond problems and issues in my love life, I was still trying to make a living, pay bills, and make ends meet, but by this time, my job had all but stopped giving raises, and this brought a lot of tension in the workplace. I was in a daily battle with this one guy at my job—that story alone is a book. I don't know if it was the enemy trying to break me or what. All I know is that I wasn't breakin' for nothin'. I had been through too much and had come too far, and God had carried me too far to leave me.

This was a very challenging time in my life. I had to keep the pieces together. I remember this one day when I had to hustle to finish work in Fort Lauderdale and drive to Miami to pick up my children. I texted my mom these words: "I know how to struggle.

I need to know how to be blessed." Little did I know she would save and record that text, as she had so many others. I've told you throughout the book that my mom and I have always been close, that I've always felt comfortable communicating and sharing my deepest thoughts with her, so we did a lot of texting during this time in my life.

When cell phones were becoming all the rage in the late nineties, I hadn't rushed to get one. I just didn't feel the need. But once my oldest son was born, I saw the need and wanted to always be available for anything concerning him, so I finally got one. So since he was with my mom, she and I would text each other regularly.

I shared many of my thoughts with my mom, almost like I was relaying my struggles and the things I was going through as they were happening in real time. She was the receiving ear, but I had no idea she was saving all these texts—phrases and expressions like the one I mentioned previously. These were thoughts describing what I was feeling at a particular time. She was saving them. She copied them from her phone to a notebook and would sometimes say, "You should put these in a book." So for those of you who may be wondering how these words, thoughts, and expressions come from me, someone who is usually a quiet, reserved person, that is how. I never thought about a book. I was just doing what I always did—just being me, having deep thoughts but never really speaking them. But I was texting them to my mom, who saved them over several years, all in hopes that some of these words would one day help people going through the same thing or going through their own struggles.

One thing about our calling: we don't choose it; rather, it chooses us. It could be right in your face, but you may miss it because it feels natural and comes so easily. That's what writing is to me. It's something I've always done. I guess that may be looked at as a good sign you have something, whatever that something is—because it feels easy to you, like second nature; you enjoy doing it; and it helps you and others around you. So you may never know what your calling is. Just stay true to yourself and follow your heart, and God will take care of the rest.

STRENGTHENING FAITH

"Ma, I really feel I'm at this particular church for a reason. The hardships of just maintaining are all for a reason. It's a reason I'm so heavily involved in this ministry and sowing so much." This is what I texted at another turning point in my life.

I was looking for a church family for me and my kids and wanted to start doing things the right way—someday get married and live the right way. The new young lady I was with at the time knew someone from a good Bible-based Christ-first Baptist church, and although I'd been baptized in a church, gone to church regularly with my mom and dad as a li'l' git, read my Bible, and even gone to Christian schools, I didn't know about all the denominations and what they meant—Baptist, Pentecostal, Episcopalian, Evangelical. All I knew was that the Bible was the word of God and Jesus was my Savior. So we visited the church. First time I was there, I felt an immediate connection like I'd never felt before. It felt so real, and it felt like home, like heaven. So we joined about a month later, and we were all baptized: me, her, my son, and her son.

I've always had a servant's heart, always wanted to help people, so immediately I got involved in the ministries. I was dedicating my time because I had so much to give back. I mentioned earlier that I was coaching Little League football, but I never told you how that all started. Well, I feel it came to me because of strengthening my faith. I was not only coaching but coaching at a neighborhood park, which gave me the feeling of giving back.

There I was in the check-cashing store, not looking for a coaching job but always thinking about football, and I overheard this guy talking about his team. It seemed like things were beginning to click for me, so I asked the guy the process for getting involved in coaching. He was coaching the Western Tigers, who'd been rivals when I played football at Lauderdale Lakes Vikings as a child. They always had been rivals, and they still are, but under different conditions. I'd have liked to coach at the park where'd I played as a kid, but I was more interested in helping my community than winning a Super Bowl. Sunland Park was in my community, so that's the park where I chose to volunteer. I loved it! I was around my first love again, football. I knew the game in and out—I played it, studied it—and now I was coaching it. I was also helping kids along the way.

My first year of coaching, we didn't win one game, but I know that I reached a lot of kids who needed to be inspired. I was giving back to my community the only way I could at that time, giving my service. I coached defense for about four years, but sooner than I'd wanted, the time conflicted with my making a living, so I had to leave coaching and volunteering. It was a good experience and served as a haven from all the stress that everyday life brought.

I was also active in my church and was beginning to get to know the people, as they were my church family now, my church home. I was happy my kids now had a church they could grow up in and I had a place to fellowship, worship, and serve. It was what I needed to help me in my walk with Christ.

One day, after church, I heard our pastor mention a meeting on Monday evenings. I was curious because I wanted to do this all the way, so I went one night. I didn't know that I was getting ready to meet a group of men who would change the rest of my life. See, I had my views about church; I felt that it was too judgmental, hypocritical, and phony and that it was all about money, until I saw the movie *The Passion of the Christ* a few years back. That movie opened my eyes to a lot. I was watching it with my children, and the oldest asked, "Where do we go when we die?" I saw that as the perfect opening to lead my son to Christ and salvation. So I did.

I explained it all to him, and then he accepted Christ as his Savior and got salvation. That took a huge burden off my shoulders because that's all I want for my children. I don't care much about them being rich and receiving all the accolades that come with being successful. That's important, but what I want most for them is to become men who love the Lord.

Back to the Monday-night meeting. I walked into one of the most powerful rooms I had ever been in in my life. It was known as the MOB, a men's ministry full of men who had been in all kinds of situations and were trying to be better, do better, and live for the Lord. The first night I went, I'd left my Bible in my ride, so I walked out to get it, but when I went back, the door was locked. I was new, so I didn't have the sense to ask someone how to get back in or just go in the front of the church to the meeting, so I went home. But I went back the next week because I wanted to see what MOB was all about—as it's not to be confused in any way with the negative street slang that shares the same acronym: money over b—— (out of respect for the positive frame here, I'll leave the rest to your imagination). From the moment I went into that group, its members received me, made me feel welcomed, listened to me when I spoke, and never judged me. They fed me food and fed me the word of God and had only one rule: "What is said here stays here."

All kinds of topics were discussed in this ministry, and before guys spoke and opened up to get help with whatever situations they were dealing with, there had to be trust—they had to feel comfortable opening up without worrying that what they shared would come back on them.

This was different from regular service on Sunday. This was a small concentrated group of men only, helping one another become better men, helping one another lead their families and finally reverse the cycle for which black men have historically been known. I had never been around a group of men with that much positivity, with that much of God concentrated in one area. We are all made in His image, His likeness, so you get a group of men, the heads of families, together, and that's a lot of God power in one room.

All meetings started and ended in prayer. I owe a huge amount of credit to how God used that ministry to help a young man get to the next spiritual level of his life. I consider the loyal men of MOB as my lifetime spiritual brothers, and I love and thank every one of y'all for everything. You gentlemen know who you are.

LEARNING ABOUT YOURSELF

"I'm right within, but I'm messed up on the outside." It should be the other way around.

Before I share this part, I must say that everyone I've mentioned in this book has been influential in my life and there's only love being expressed. I said everything must change. I'm proud to say that my dad worked out his issues and struggles and that our relationship has improved in the past few years, and one thing's for sure—he's definitely a good granddad.

If we're gonna be real with ourselves, we have to admit when we're wrong, and I've been wrong in the past. Earlier, I mentioned that some years ago, I started a family with a young lady who had my second son, and began another family with a young lady I had known several years before. Although my baby boy's mom and I were already having serious problems, problems that had been there from the start and were the cause of our breakup, this was wrong. Regardless of the reason, it was wrong. I won't make excuses. I can deal only with me and how I handle any given situation and then try to go forward.

This relationship I started outside my family and didn't last long. It started with dishonesty and ended the same way, mainly because of its existence. It never should have been. As it turned out, I was not the father of the children she claimed; she and I did not have a family.

We all need time to heal and mend feelings. It takes time and patience to build back trust between people, but to do and say spiteful things to try to bring about the suffering of someone who may have disappointed you or caused you anger or maybe even pain will result in your never growing as a person. You can never will your pain or suffering on someone else; it just doesn't work that way. No one will ever feel your pain the way you've felt it, even if you do the very same thing to them that they did to you. We've all done somebody wrong at some point in our lives, and if people continue down that path, keep doing wrong and never turning away from it, then it's for sure they have not given themselves to righteousness. When you see your wrongs, own them, and turn away from them, then all you need to do is be thankful that God already paid the ultimate price long ago to be sure you were forgiven.

When your past wrongs are kept in front of you, and you are constantly put in a position where everything you do for the people you care about and love, especially your children, is diminished, then you know throughout that entire relationship, you are a target.

I once read this in a book: "The attacks on your life have more to do with who you might be in the future than who you have been in the past." That's so real for me. You see, you have to always know that God has already forgiven you for any wrongs you have done or will do, so you can't allow anything or anyone to trap you in a web, because all they want and all they can ever see are your past mistakes—as though they are perfect, and as we know, none of us are. So all you can do is continue to pray for those people and not accept their efforts to block your progress.

The analogy of boiling water, carrots, eggs, and coffee beans comes from the speech of a student who spoke at my sister's high school graduation. It stuck with me and comes to mind often. There are three kinds of people in the world. The boiling water represents life and the challenges we go through either because of another person or by ourselves, but we all have to go through something. The carrot represents the first person. They start out life strong and firm, but when they go through life, the pressure breaks them down and makes them weak, the way a carrot starts hard and ends up soft after being boiled. The people we may liken to eggs start off giving, flexible, and loving, but as with eggs that are cold, the trials of life make people cold, hard, and unrelenting—hardened in the heart. The eggshell is hard in order to protect the vulnerability inside. The coffee beans represent the kind of people who go through fiery trials and not only don't break form but remain unchanged by their surroundings; they give of themselves as the trials of life bring out the best in them. Like coffee beans, these people keep their form, but the water turns brown and fills the whole room with its pleasant aroma. So it's not about what happens to us; it's about how we let what happens affect us. But at some point, we must let go of the past and forgive, in between our healing and learning to trust again. "Unconditional love holds no records of wrongs about true love," and the Bible speaks to that in 1 Corinthians 13.

Unfortunately, some people never let go of the past, and if there are children involved, this can have damaging effects and make a big impact on how those children are raised, especially when the parents are not raising them together. Often, the parent who has custody has the advantage when it comes to how the children will think of and respect the other parent. Obviously, a lot of what the children see or hear will come from the parent with custody. It doesn't matter whether the other parent is supporting financially or spending quality time with the kids, especially in a father-son relationship—the father doesn't stand a chance when most of what the child knows of him is based solely on the unyielding scorned heart of the other parent. So whatever may have caused you and your mate to separate, no matter who hurt who, you have to let go of the pain and move forward for the sake and love of the children. On the other hand, I salute those parents who allow their children to grow in love from both parents by not speaking negatively of each other.

In situations where my intentions were genuine and right, I sometimes just went about things the wrong way. I wanted to have a family—always did—and I knew how important a man's presence in the home is, so I really wanted to have my children under one roof and raise them in a family environment. But I was going about it the wrong way—my way instead of God's way. I was creating families by bringing children into the world first and trying to make a family second.

We live and learn. One thing I learned was that I needed to break from relationships and just chill by myself for a while—let things settle and clear my head from all that had taken place in the past few years: the arguing back and forth, the breaking up and making up, the barrage of insults, the disrespect, and all the turmoil that my relationship had been full of those last few years. I needed time to get myself right because obviously I wasn't ready for a real relationship; I wasn't being serious about birth control; and, most of all, my oldest son, who I was raising, was a major part of everything I did.

Until my second son, I'd never had my oldest son around any young lady other than his mother and family members. The two women I've been talking about up to this point were the only two I had around him because my main interest was having a family and I didn't want to confuse him. Not to imply that it was a contest in any way, but there were more than emotional ties to consider. Children were involved, and decisions had to be made carefully. As time went on, I began to feel that all the going back and forth between the two of these women wasn't good. It started to become exactly what I'd been trying to avoid—confusion. Thankfully, he spent most of his time at my mom's. Although, in his mind, wherever I was always represented home to him. I picked him up every day after school, met my mom every night so she could take him to school the next morning, and spent every single weekend with him.

When you have been raised to know God, you get to a point in your life where you need to trust Him more. I started reading the Bible more, getting further into God's Word, and I was beginning to see a lot of my wrongs more clearly. I became celibate for a little while and tried to hear more of what God wanted to say to me regarding a family.

When you're in your walk with Christ, daily problems can make your walk always feel new, and it can be difficult at times to know the difference between what His will is for you and what yours is. This is when it gets complicated, because the relationship itself was a very difficult one. Although two people may want a family, as in this case, but two people may not be ready at the same time to sacrifice and to put the past behind them. Our past was full of turmoil and ugliness, and I knew I couldn't do—and didn't want—any more of the same. No one should allow themselves to live in constant disharmony with anyone, for any reason, ever. So with prayer and spiritual counseling at my request, we tried to pick up where we'd left off and rebuild our family. For the first few months, things were going smoothly. We were going to church and worshiping together as a family, sharing as a family, and then, out of nowhere, some old behavior resurfaced—but no matter, things went wrong. We had a bad week, and then, suddenly, bags were packed, and she left. It seemed that none of the prayer and worship our family had engaged in during that time had any impact.

I know many men have been in this scene before, and I would've understood it more had this been a different time, but during this time, I was walking right, being real, and waiting to celebrate and ring in the New Year as a family. Who knows what our next step might have been? Well, it didn't add up that way. Women sometimes have an agenda that men are not always privy to, and obviously, this was the case. I'm the type of person who respects people's choices. She'd chosen to leave at a time when were talking and working through issues, and I had to respect her wishes. So I did not ask her to come back.

This time was different, though. This time I felt lifted, and I felt a certain joy. Yes, I would miss not having my baby boy living with me, would be coming home without him there. Even so, I was more prepared for her to move on this time. This was a new feeling I had never experienced in this relationship, and I feel it was because of my new relationship with my Lord. I was walking in the Word more, drawing closer to and believing more in the power of prayer. The way I saw it was this had to be God's will, not mine. I felt that if a woman could leave so easily when things were going smoothly, then what would she do when things got rough?

So a month after she walked out, there I was, going forward and spending time with the Lord and with both my sons. Those were the days full of insults. I could handle them, but I didn't understand the hate: she'd wanted to leave, I let her, she got what she wanted, and I was moving on with my life. So why was she spewing so much anger? I didn't push to find out. Disrespectful language is one thing among adults, but that she used it in front of children—my son and our son—was a little hard for me to handle. We all know, to a black man, being called *boy* is the lowest of insults, and I think certain women know this and use it to degrade a man and drive in the nail. I didn't like knowing that my son had to be raised around all that drama and those choice words. I don't know how I would have made it had it not been for my faith and love for God.

FORWARD CHALLENGES

There we were, trying to raise our son separately. Then, about a month after the breakup, I was leaving our son's birthday party and got a call. It was the call a man is never prepared for, especially after a breakup, but it's one that causes him to think over every step he makes from that point forward—immediately. Yep, you got it: she was pregnant.

I didn't want to bring another child into the world without being married, but sometimes, when you live together before marriage, things happen. Although I'd tried to do everything on my part to avoid this, neither of us had been careful enough. I wasn't ready financially, so waiting to have another child was something on which we had both agreed.

Well, of course, now she wanted to come back, but this was a very toxic relationship, and it seemed like this coming and going was becoming a pattern. I did not want that. I never understood the reason for getting back together in the first place, and then to leave after a few months, when she was expecting—because women know long before anyone else when they are pregnant—none of it made sense to me. We weren't seeing eye to eye at all, so we kept our distance during this pregnancy.

I never set out to hurt anyone, especially either of those two young ladies, but within the walls in which we live, it's not always what it looks like to outsiders. We all know that sometimes people will distort the truth to gain favor or empathy from those same outsiders. It's always easier to attack a man's integrity because the world usually sees him as the wrong one in a relationship, and to be fair, more times than not, he is. But no matter what a woman does, says, or pretends to be, regardless of whether she's the cause of problems, she is seldom viewed as the deserter or wrong one. I took both relationships seriously and tried at different times to make a family with each woman. I believed so much that I was doing the right thing that I went to spiritual counseling with each one, as I feel more confident about taking my concerns to prayerful counseling than to opinionated friends. Unfortunately, I was with them back and forth, but like I said, it was at different times. I was praying to make the right choice through it all, hoping that at the end of all the confusion, some good would come. I found that neither relationship was right for me and what I was trying to have for my life and my children. When you decide to start over, to leave everything in the past and start new, truth has to be one of the most important things you build on. It seemed that I was the only one to realize this each time I tried to get back with either of these young ladies.

You may wonder why I'm sharing these events, and as I said before, I'm only expressing and sharing in this book in hopes that my words will help others with their struggles. I'm sure you can relate, regardless of your gender. I'm sure you have found yourself in a time of doubt, a time when you didn't know where to turn, when you felt every decision you were making on your own was the wrong one. I just want to express how important it is for us to know God's love for us and to love ourselves. If we don't love ourselves, we're not ever gonna feel worthy of being loved and receiving the love another person has to give. I'm thankful to my God for loving me because I didn't always love myself. When we love ourselves, we can confront any fear, pain, disappointment, bitterness, or hatred we're holding on to because honest love drives out all fear. I think that once we confront our feelings, we're free to live because we're no longer in bondage or shackles.

DEALING WITH BAGGAGE

Sometimes we walk into people's lives while they are carrying baggage they've been holding on to since before we even knew them. I don't pretend to be no head doctor, no analyst or nothin'. I'm just learning to be a good listener, especially to people who matter to me.

Leftover baggage too often becomes bitterness—when people don't forgive others or let go of pain they may have experienced. But change needs to start with them, no matter what may have happened in any past relationship. Learning to forgive and forget past pain must first start on the inside. If not, someone else ends up bearing the burden. Nobody likes rejection—it's not a good feeling—but I've learned that it's a part of life. We can' t let it discourage us and deny ourselves a blessing because we're afraid—that's fear. When we can't forgive others for things from our pasts, we only mess up things for ourselves. All this attitude does is keep us hostage to the wrong that we feel has been done to us, and it makes us miserable. It causes us to develop a negative outlook and believe that everybody is out to hurt us, and this isn't healthy. When we keep ourselves locked inside this negative way of thinking, it gets inside and consumes us. It takes root and, like a wild plant, can choke us. It becomes who we are, in misery, so we pass on that misery that so often is attached to guilt.

We have to realize that problems are solved from within. We have to fix ourselves, and to do that, we have to first love ourselves.

Hopefully, most of us have never been incarcerated or behind any kind of bars, but we have all been in prison in our minds. When we forgive, we're free to live because we understand that we have done wrong and were once held hostage to our wrongs but that someone showed us love so that we could quiet all the noise. I was that someone.

Life shows us that people are not perfect. Life isn't perfect, and we're gonna feel pain, but that's why God is there for us. He loves us despite ourselves and our wrongs. He takes the pain away and replaces it with joy. It still amazes me that the Almighty loved me, as messed up as I was. When we accept how much He loves us, we begin to fix the problems within ourselves. We understand we're not as good as we thought we were, and that's when we take control of our lives, instead of letting others control us by the things we allow them to do to us. But it's gotta start with us.

Thank God the baby was born on time and healthy and I was now the father of three boys. I was very thankful for three healthy boys, but soon, the reality of more child support slapped me in the face. My job had not given raises for almost four years, taxes and insurance were rising, gas was high, and I was still driving a gas-guzzler van. My lawn business had all but ended because not having seed money for repairs and backup equipment had left me hangin' when normal repairs were needed. I lost a lot of customers who were in Miami, but I had to let them go because it was too much wear and tear on a vehicle traveling from county to county every day. I was constantly falling behind on my rent, and I still had my oldest son, who I still had to feed and provide for, who was depending on what I brought home.

I'm not looking for any special understanding or sympathy here. We all have financial obligations and deeds to perform when we have children, and no one knows that better than mothers. They are usually the custodial parents—except in my case, my oldest son lived with me, I was given full charge. Therefore, like all young custodial single parents, I needed the support of my son's mother and my family, and I'm happy to give credit where its due, I received support from them both and I thank God every day for that.

My oldest son's mom was around and involved in decisions for and about him. Whether it was a school conference or doctor's appointment, or if it was just a matter of behavioral issues, she was there and never charged blame, because she knew the importance of our working together for the good. My mother and other family members on both sides were also there for us. Whenever I went to a family function, my son would be right there with me, so he was no stranger to either my mom's or my dad's family.

My routine was that I would pick my son up from school, cook dinner, help with homework, and, most times, make it to church for our Monday-night men's meetings. There, they made allowances for him because they knew I was a single dad. Afterward, we would meet my mom when she left her nighttime teaching job, and my son would be fast asleep. He spent the night with her because, as I mentioned earlier, my job started too early for me to take him to school. This arrangement worked because at least I was with him for most of his waking hours. Although my mom had her hands full with her own life, had her financial responsibilities, and was a big help to me personally, my son was my responsibility. I supported him and didn't burden my mom with his needs, but child support was hitting my paycheck hard, and it didn't leave much room for planning.

I don't keep track of how much time people spend with their kids, because as long as the time spent is quality time, that's what's important. We know there are some men who don't pay child support or spend time with their kids, and then there are some who pay child support and see their kids only on holidays or birthdays. I'm not faulting or criticizing anyone, because everyone's situation is different—no one knows what drama anyone may be dealing with. But there are fathers who do the right thing and are treated the same as those who don't, and for that, I do fault and criticize the system and the custodial parent for not making a distinction. We should not all be placed in the same box when it comes to our children or child support.

I've always spent time with my kids, as I'm sure many men have, and I spent the time because I wanted to, not because I was ordered by the state. But the system doesn't recognize this, and oftentimes, neither does the custodial parent. When my boys spent their designated weekends with me, everything was shared, and money was equally spent, even though child support was still going to pull that same big chunk from my check. The system didn't recognize that, and neither did the custodial parent. After child support, bills, food, and gas, there was basically nothin' left. There were times when I spent more on my kids who were not in the home than on the one who was. Thankfully, I managed, and my son who lived with me never had to do without. It still amazes me to this day how many happy memories he has from the days when the two of us would just hang around together. He's always reminding me of places we went, TV shows we watched, stories we read, movies we saw, and Bible lessons we talked about together, so in this case, money truly wasn't everything. My boys were also happy when they were there. I could tell because they never wanted our weekends to end—neither did I—and for that, I was happy. The frustration I felt from the unfairness of the system and the constant feeling of disrespect from a scornful custodial parent temporarily went away during those times when I was with my boys.

Although after I separated from the two youngest boys' mom I was always able to see them, never denied my time with them, it was always met with a lot of friction. It was very difficult to be in my two youngest boys' lives, which is unfortunate for the children, because they didn't ask to be here. Parents must put personal feelings aside for the best interests of the child.

NO MORE GUILT

n my young life, I had felt enough guilt over the years to last a lifetime: guilt over not having been in the backyard to save my uncle, guilt over not having finished college, and guilt over having brought children into the world under less-than-ideal situations. But no more guilt. I had held on to enough guilt, and I was finally letting it go, so I wasn't gonna let others hold their guilt over my head. As I mentioned, my guilt lifted the more I realized how much God loved me.

I was in a tight spot financially, and I was really trying to change my ways, so I wasn't going back to the block to make money. Even though I had to make ends meet one way or another, I wasn't going backward—not to my old relationships, not to my old habits. I was going forward. I wasn't gonna bend over to sell out, wasn't gonna bend my morals and values, and wasn't gonna bend over backward to please the next person, because all of that is control.

The enemy thrives on putting us in compromising positions, hoping that we will break and give in one way or another. But I had to hold my own in everything; I've had to all my life, and I never took handouts from anyone, never wanted any. Not that I was too proud—I just knew in the back of my mind that God always had me, that He would never let me go. Even when it was dark, I knew He was with me. I never had much, but I knew whatever I had, it was authentic and true because I had earned it from the ground up.

I had been to my rock bottom, been through my hell, and I was still here. I figured if things in my past hadn't destroyed me, then nothing would, now that I understood more that God is my protector. I knew that so long as He was with me, I would be OK. I had no reason to give up, no reason to fold, and I was too stubborn to break. So I just held on as struggles continued, but no more guilt. "Joy comes in the morning," and I had seen a lot of long, long dark nights, but I knew that with God, things don't always stay the same; change would come (Psalm 30:5).

As my journey continues, I'm happy and proud to say that the young ladies I mentioned throughout this book, from the mother of my first sweet baby boy, whose life was too short, to my oldest son's mother, have since moved on and are doing well; as for my youngest boy's mom, hopefully she will find her happiness. I wish them all the best, I'm still working on my mine.

TWO NEW PRECIOUS CHALLENGES

God must see something in me, because I was blessed with two more beautiful, healthy children, a set of twin girls, two more of His children to love. I had never experienced having a daughter, let alone two at the same time, but they were two little precious infant baby girls, two little princesses, and I had new challenges in front of me. I had been doing things my way, and although I had let go of a lot of ways from my past, there was still more to be cleaned up. So I took a big step back, got out of the way, and asked God to take control, to lead. I was used to being the one to make something happen, taking the initiative, but not this time. This time, I was ready to sit back and just let God.

TURNING A CORNER

I met her the same week my grandma passed. It was a very rough time for me. I had lost someone whom I loved dearly, so meeting someone new right at that time, I felt like God was sending her my way. Here was someone with a fresh new attitude and a positive way of thinking. It made me think back to when I realized that even though I'd lost my firstborn son in death, I'd gained Christ in my life. I lost my son, but He gave me His son so that I could live.

She was a member of my church—and very involved. I did parking lot service. It's something I've always enjoyed, and it was natural for me, out on the street and around the people. I like to take what I've learned in church and go outside the church walls and give it back because not everyone comes into the church. Inside, we sing praise, and everything is good, but then it's back to reality and all the problems of our world. So immediately I gravitated outside the church walls to serve.

I learned later that she had been eyeing me for several months, and when I saw her, I was curious about what could come from this. But I never really had a clue. Remember I wasn't looking for someone at this time. So she finally expressed her interest to a mutual friend, and he called me, told me about her, and said I should call her. We started talking and moving forward. I was totally up front with her about my life and where I was in it—yes, even about the baby on the way, because I didn't want to get involved while a woman was pregnant with my child. I was honest with her, because if she was the one, I wanted everything to be out in the open. I told her I was a blue-collar workingman who drove a van, had a two-bedroom apartment, and was living paycheck to paycheck. I wanted it all on the table. I wanted the decision to be hers to go forward with a man in my situation; it had to be what she wanted.

No one understands what one person may see in another or needs to see. I just always hoped people would see who I really was underneath all the rubble of what life had given. We started dating, praying, and worshiping together, and we talked about a lot of things. I shared things that were important to me—my beliefs, my goals, and, one of the most important, my love for my children and how I treasure the bond I have with them. I take being a father very seriously. I may not have gone about it the right way, but being a father has a lot of meaning, and I wanted to share what I have with my children with the right person at the right time. I hoped one day to give them as much of the wholeness of a family as I could under the circumstances. When the baby was born, I told her. I had another son.

She and I were getting close, and early in our relationship, we both proved our loyalty by being there for each other in the toughest of times. We prayed through them together and asked for strength, guidance, and an uplifting spirit, and I began to share more of who I was with her. She's a person with a good spirit inside. That's what drew me to her—the soul inside her. Later in our relationship, I had to have hernia surgery. The whole time, she was by my side. It was the same as when she needed me; I was right there with her and happy to be there.

We were both two strong people, loving each other and dealing with situations from our pasts. She had two great children whom she had raised together with their father in a twenty-year relationship. I still had young children who I was helping to raise outside my home, so that was a challenge. Not to mention there were people from our pasts who didn't want us to be with anyone else. Needless to say, the beginning stages of our relationship weren't smooth.

We took it one day at a time because we truly believed that we had the most important things: a relationship with God and hopes for a new beginning. Here I was, a young single father who didn't have much to offer in the way of material things—no house, not a lot of money, no flashy life at all—but I was the man in her life at a time when she needed someone strong to love and support her. So apparently that was more important to her than how much money I didn't have, because she was so real. And I was real. I was a man who had experienced things many men twice his age never had or would. I had nurtured, tended to, and helped care for a premature baby and then lost that same baby in death; had cared for my other son from birth; and had lived on my own for a number of years, supporting myself and my child by working two jobs and never, ever accepting government assistance. I had also owned my own business, so yes, I am a man who made mistakes, yet I had God in my life now, and my relationship with Him was stronger than ever before.

I knew that whatever I was gonna need going forward, I was covered. It all just felt right, so I was starting to believe that all of this must have been a part of God's plan—that she must have been the wife I'd asked God for—so I proposed. We got married a few months later, the first time for either of us.

Our first year of marriage was filled with feelings of loving and caring for each other. It was new yet also characterized by the challenges of starting with a ready-made family. Relationships between black men and black women are one of the toughest challenges we face, along with being parents. Some call it a battle of the flesh and the spirit. But we are spirits first, living in physical bodies to manifest spiritual duties in physical world. So there are two sides to our spirits, the higher self (God) and the lower self (satan), and we have to learn to control the lower self to keep it from rising and breaking the balance. Men and women complement each other and must create a balance between them. This is important because many relationships have distractions from the past, and when children are involved, they become more challenging.

Our individual balance and the balance between ourselves and our mates compose the foundation of our relationships. Then there are negative energies and spirits that work against us just because we are the people of God, and the black man and black woman together form the key component of the black family: unity. So through God and prayer, we're presently taking this day by day and learning as we go along.

Like I said, this book wasn't planned. It was written as I lived my life and had experiences. After I left college and moved back home, my mom and I started something that even now carries me through my days. It started with me and my mom declaring that we had something to be thankful to God for each day. We would write it and leave it for the other to see each morning before we left for our day. Then, later, the note writing turned into texting. It turned out to be over a period of five to six years of my texting her my thoughts. That's a lot of thoughts. So from my mom saving and recording them unknown to me came the foundation of this book.

Writing has always been a gift in my family. My grandma on my mom's side was a writer. I never met her, but she must have passed that gift on to me. My aunt was a writer, as well as my uncle, who has written a book and published a collection of my grandmother's poetry. So I guess maybe it's in me.

My mom decided to present our conversations to a publisher, just finding ways to use my experiences and expressions to help and inspire others who might be dealing with some of the same struggles. The publisher liked what she saw and suggested we put some of my affirmations, thoughts, and beliefs in a book. So here it is. All through this book are experiences and lessons I know other people are dealing with and just might not have had the opportunity to express.

You may be able to relate to things I've shared here. Or maybe you can't. But whatever stage of life you're in now, I pray this book has been helpful. I don't have all the answers—I don't even have answers to my own life. I'm just a young man, so I'm still learning as I go, but I know to go to God for my answers. This book is no more than personal experiences, not a guide for people to follow to live their lives by. But I know this fo' sho: We are exactly what we think of ourselves. Nothing can stop us but ourselves, and there is nothing we can't do.

A limited mind and limited faith bring limited results. So have unlimited faith, and open your mind to new possibilities. All things are possible with God. He's real, He's love, and He's good. It's evident to me what can be done through His power, all the way from what we as blacks have accomplished down to folks closer to me, right here at home and in my personal life:

We have had our first black president, and my maternal grandmother (who I never knew) prayed and believed in it so much that she wrote a poem titled "Why Not a Negro for President" sixty-seven years before it happened. Following an accident at his own landscaping company, my granddad overcame being in a full-body cast to find a way to provide for his family, becoming known as the Snowball Man after building a homemade truck with an icebox on the back and selling snowballs and other goodies from it (I wish it had been during my time, ha ha). That's the power of God. We overcame many struggles and demons. My dad went to school and became the first black man in the area to receive a mortgage broker's license, helping to educate people about getting home loans and then putting his own family in a respectable home as well. That's the power of God. My mom taught students and counseled with so much passion that they come back years later to say thank you. That's teaching with the power of God. We had the first male in our family earn a master's degree against all odds and come back home to raise our family. That's the power of God. We had the first in our family to go onstage and do live comedy, after having survived the Vietnam War as a marine on the front line, as well as a quadruple heart attack and surgery. That's the power of God. My granddad came from the Bahamas with nothing, built a home from the ground up, and started a family in a new place. That's the power of God. We have overcome the plight of drugs and disease and still turned out to be great fathers to our kids. That's the power of God. We have survived the loss of both a daughter and a granddaughter in a fire and still have had enough love to give to anyone who meets or knows us. That's the power of God. We survived cancer, and we've battled the disease of Alzheimer's and open-heart surgery—all through the power of God. We were diagnosed with sickle cell and grew up healthy and loving and continued to be strong through every hospital stay. That's the power of God. We overcame the death of two husbands and still raised three children and put a daughter through college. That's the power of God. We literally died on the hospital table during heart surgery and survived to tell the story to bring others to Christ. And there's so much more I've lived and seen in my life, in my family, that is through the power of God, and it's because of His power today that I'm here writing this book.

So don't let anyone tell you what you can't do. Never give up in the struggle, because blessings are always right around the corner. My struggle was finding truth; I always knew it because it had been revealed to me a while before. Anything true and real we know has always been revealed to us—it just takes time for us to recognize it in this body. As I wrote this book, my truth slowly presented itself to me.

This book isn't meant to be just about struggles. Yes, I've had them—financial struggles; relationship struggles; fatherhood struggles; growing-up struggles, both educational and spiritual—and I'm still struggling. I know there are more struggles just around the corner. But this book is more about my blessings, because although my biggest struggle was finding out the meaning of life and why I am here, it's always about the many blessings we sometimes miss. This book is mostly about how God used all those trials I underwent to reach me, bring me back, and keep me close to Him.

I had problems with commitment, relationships, jobs, and school—and no excuses, but the ways of the world can confuse us.

So much respect is given based on how much money, how many women, and how many material things we have—cars, houses, jewelry, clothes, and so on.

Things of that nature—the material things—aren't solid. We can't stand on them when the world around us is crumbling. Those things give way and come and go; they don't make us who we are. There's nothing wrong with money, but it ain't nothin' but paper that humankind has put so much value on. It doesn't make us who we are, so don't worship it and give up everything you are to gain it. Worship God.

Yes, money can get us a lot of things in life. It's very important in this world, as life can be difficult without it, but the power that all things come from, the power that enables us to gain things, is available to us, with us, and alive within us—it is of God. We can't go back and undo things in our lives that we don't want to be there anymore; there's nothing we can do to change the past. We can only change ourselves to change our futures and learn from our pasts. I'm doing that.

What I've learned is that the real blessing is not rejecting the struggle but accepting something that has to be. Blessings and struggles go hand in hand; you can't have one without the other. The struggles help us appreciate the blessings even more, and going through the struggles with a blessed state of mind is what gives us the strength to endure until more blessings are brought to our lives. Our blessings come when we focus on what we want to happen instead of what we don't want to happen. Recognizing that we are in fact blessed simply because we were created by the Most High doesn't mean the struggle is over; it means that as we grow, further our progress, and reach a higher level of consciousness, we will face new struggles as a result of growth.

The good thing is I'm learning to look at struggles differently. They come with the territory of surging forward and going beyond the restrictions that have been strategically set in an environment that doesn't promote natural, spiritual, and universal truth. The blessing is life in itself, the concrete relationships we form with people while we experience the journey. It's the realization of mind over matter, which helps us understand our current circumstances and maneuver through them in ways that benefit us and those around us.

Struggles are a constant reminder that I must stay close to God, the creator of all and the power that holds all things together; a reminder of my ancestors, who paved the way for me as the originals of humanity, who died in my place so that I could have life; and a reminder to never forget about the Christ factor that lives inside the true called people of God and to keep my love walk intact as I move through this third-dimensional realm.

I'm a man, and my experiences have shown me that I can mess things up, as many have before me, but they also let me know I am capable of great things—that I alone have the choice to allow a good or evil motive to dwell within me, to continually live in either a hellish or an abundant truth. I've seen both in my life. I was in heaven seeing the birth of my son, and I was brought right down to hell when I went through the process of burying him. At any moment, we can decide who and what we are, and we can take the necessary steps that lead us to a place where we are striving to be.

We can shape our own reality with our minds because the laws and principles that govern us, the laws of nature, never change. Put energy into thinking about what you want instead of what you don't want. We must keep grateful, thankful hearts for everything that is because we have a major part in its existence. Good results are sure to come, so trust in God Almighty, as that's the surest source we know since being in our mothers' wombs.

My prayer is that through your struggles, you learn how to be blessed and to find your truth.

One love. Be blessed.

April 17, 2021: I started writing this book in 2014. Much has changed since then—perhaps that is another book. But what has not changed, I am proud to say, is my strong belief in God. My business is thriving, my family is healthy, my two youngest sons are growing strong, and my oldest son is a man now and will be leaving for college this year. I am blessed. I continue to go through the storm, but the one thing that's better now, when I come out of challenging encounters with people and situations, is a greater appreciation for the woman I am with today. She is my love, my friend and we have each other's back. She is the mother of my twin girls, the little princesses I introduced as infants earlier in the book. She and I are together and on a journey to make our lives and all our children's lives better. I also have a greater appreciation for who I am because I know who I am, and I am a person who lives for peace.

Printed in the United States
by Baker & Taylor Publisher Services